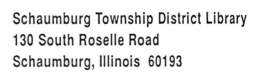

Senior
Cats

ANIMAL PLANET ♥ PET CARE LIBRARY

SHEILA WEBSTER BONEHAM, Ph.D.

Senior Cats

Project Team
Editor: Mary E. Grangeia
Copy Editor: Stephanie Fornino
Interior Design: Leah Lococo Ltd. and Stephanie Krautheim
Design Layout: Patricia Escabi

T.F.H. Publications
President/CEO: Glen S. Axelrod
Executive Vice President: Mark E. Johnson
Publisher: Christopher T. Reggio
Production Manager: Kathy Bontz

Discovery Communications, Inc. Book Development Team
Marjorie Kaplan, President, Animal Planet Media
Carol LeBlanc, Vice President, Licensing
Elizabeth Bakacs, Vice President, Creative Services
Peggy Ang, Vice President, Animal Planet Marketing
Caitlin Erb, Licencing Specialist

T.F.H. Publications, Inc.
One TFH Plaza
Third and Union Avenues
Neptune City, NJ 07753

Printed and bound in China
07 08 09 10 11 1 3 5 7 9 8 6 4 2

Library of Congress Cataloging-in-Publication Data
Boneham, Sheila Webster, 1952-
    Senior cats / Sheila Webster Boneham.
            p. cm.
    Includes bibliographical references and index.
    ISBN 978-0-7938-3781-6 (alk. paper)
  1. Cats. 2. Cats—Aging. 3. Cats—Health. 4. Veterinary geriatrics. I. Title.
    SF447.B62 2007
    636.8—dc22
                                    2007005382

This book has been published with the intent to provide accurate and authoritative information in regard to the subject matter within. While every reasonable precaution has been taken in preparation of this book, the author and publisher expressly disclaim responsibility for any errors, omissions, or adverse effects arising from the use or application of the information contained herein. The techniques and suggestions are used at the reader's discretion and are not to be considered a substitute for veterinary care. If you suspect a medical problem consult your veterinarian.

The Leader In Responsible Animal Care For Over 50 Years!™
www.tfh.com

Table of Contents

Chapter 1

A Special

Time of Life

If cats as a species have a serious fault, it is that their lives are so much shorter than our own. You bring home a baby kitten, and it seems like the next thing you know she's a senior feline. If you adopted your cat as an adult, the days you share may seem even fewer—our Mary was a young adult when I first met her, and before we knew it she was 18 years old.

The older cat possesses a special dignity and sweetness that is every bit as precious as the cuteness of kittenhood, and she is in some ways a better companion than ever. She has the wisdom that maturity and experience bestow. She loves you, and she depends on you. And while you cannot make time stand still, in most cases you can help your cat stay healthy and active well into her teens.

With a basic guide to the steps you can take, and in partnership with your veterinarian, you can ensure that your cat remains a vital part of your life for as long as possible.

When Is Your Cat a Senior?

Individual cats, like individual people, age according to their own inner clocks. Genetics, life history, environment, and a measure of luck all play parts in determining how the body and mind respond to the passage of time. Some pet cats live well into their 20s; most live into their early teens. Some remain vital and active almost to the ends of their lives, while others are slowed by the effects of aging or other factors. Still, we can generalize to some extent.

How Many Human Years Is That?

Want to figure out your cat's approximate age in human terms? On her first birthday, she is more or less like a human being in her late teens. From then on, figure about five human years for every cat year.

Life is a process of continuous change. Your cat's first year of life is akin to a human being's childhood and adolescence, and by her first birthday, she is more or less like a person in her late teens. By about two years old, she is a fully mature adult feline equivalent of a person in her 20s. At about six years, she is much like a person in her 40s and may begin to show some early signs of aging. This is a good time to schedule a thorough examination, including some special screening tests to establish pre-geriatric baselines (see Chapter 4).

At seven or eight years of age, your cat is like a person in her

Preserve Your Memories

Life has a way of moving at such a rapid pace that we neglect to cherish the here and now, or to document the times we love. If you love your cat, keep a record of her life. Take photos of her doing her favorite things. Jot down special events and funny things she does. As Simon and Garfunkel sang in *Bookends*, "Preserve your memories, they're all that's left you."

50s and is beginning or approaching her senior phase of life, which may last another seven or eight years, or longer. With any luck, your "middle-aged" cat will maintain excellent health, although this is a time of life when disease begins to take a toll on many individuals. Your cat may begin to "look her age," or she may look much as she did at two or three years. Still, you can expect to see some signs of aging when she is between seven and ten years old.

Signs of Aging

Change is the essence of growing older, and as much as you might like your cat to stay just as she is, you will probably begin to see some physical and behavioral changes in her from seven or eight years on. Throughout this book, we will look in more detail at the ways that your cat and her life may evolve as she grows older, and what you can do to keep her healthy and happy for as long as possible.

Genetics, life history, and environment all play parts in determining how your cat will age.

Common Changes in Geriatric Cats

The following changes are typically seen in older cats. If a change in your cat comes on suddenly, is severe, or worries you, ask your veterinarian about possible causes and treatments.

Your cat's behavior may change. She may:

- be less active
- interact less with family members
- become more or less vocal
- sleep more
- hang out or hide in secluded places
- act disoriented

As your cat's metabolism changes, she may:

- gain or lose weight
- lose muscle tone and strength
- take on a "bony" feel
- develop a dull coat or dry skin
- eat and/or drink more or less
- urinate more
- defecate less frequently

- urinate and/or defecate outside the litter box

Your cat also may:

- appear stiff, sore, or lame
- lose some or all of her vision, which will be apparent if she bumps into things or fails to react to movement
- lose some or all of her hearing, which will be apparent if she doesn't react to sounds around her
- develop dental problems, including broken teeth and gum disease (symptoms include reluctance to eat, swelling or tenderness around the mouth, and/or bad breath)
- develop digestive problems, which may cause vomiting, constipation, diarrhea, gas, and/or weight loss
- become more prone to disease and infection due to her less efficient immune system

For now, let's discuss some of the general types of changes you can expect to see.

Aging cats are like aging people in many ways, which is not surprising—we are all mammals with bodies and brains that work much the same way. Your older cat may move more slowly and seem stiff, especially when she first gets up. She may have trouble going up or down stairs and may not be able to perform athletic feats that used to be second nature. Her reaction time may be slower and her eyesight and hearing less acute. Her beautiful eyes may take on a cloudy appearance, and her coat may become dry and dull and even show some signs of gray. In short, she may begin to look and move like a senior citizen.

Internal changes also occur with age. For instance, your cat's body will eventually become less efficient at regulating its own temperature, making her feel chilly when everyone else is comfy or even too warm. She can't put on extra clothing like an elderly person might, so she will look for warmer spots in the house.

Many older cats take on a "bony" feel due to loss of subcutaneous ("under the skin") fat, and the loss of that natural padding makes them seek soft places to lie down. Be sure that your cat has a comfy, clean place or two to sleep. You can purchase special orthopedic pet beds filled

FAMILY-FRIENDLY TIP

Senior Pets and Kids

Although many cats love children, the sudden arrival of a baby or child in the house can be very stressful to an older pet. It's important to keep your aging cat's special needs in mind.

Teach children to leave the cat alone unless she seeks their attention and to be gentle with her when she does. Supervise children who are too young to understand or comply. Be sure that your cat has a refuge where she can get away; if she is no longer able to jump up out of reach, you must provide her with an option. As your cat grows older, her relationship with members of your family may undergo some changes, which will depend on her individual personality and health. Remember to make decisions based on the needs and welfare of your geriatric cat.

with soft, supportive foam, but chances are your cat will prefer a cozy corner of your couch or the middle of your down comforter. Signs of aging such as slower, less agile movement or an increased preference for warm, soft places to rest are easy to observe. Other

Not All Changes Are Due to Age

Although some changes are a normal and inevitable result of growing older, others are not normal and may be symptoms of disease. Have the veterinarian examine your cat regularly, and keep her preventive care up to date. If you notice a change in her body or behavior, talk to your vet. Don't wait for your cat's next routine appointment if it's more than a week or two away— early diagnosis and treatment are essential for control of many health problems and may prolong your cat's life and quality of life.

changes are more subtle and come on so gradually that you may overlook them until they are quite pronounced. And although many changes will cause no serious difficulties for your cat, it's important to remember that cats who are middle-aged and older experience many of the same problems their human counterparts do: loss of eyesight and hearing; arthritis; heart, kidney, lung, and liver disease; dental problems; confusion; anxiety; and so on.

Some of the health problems common to elderly cats are not caused by aging, but because they take several years to develop, their symptoms appear later in life. That is why it's important to work closely with your veterinarian to diagnose and treat those conditions that may keep your cat from enjoying a long, healthy old age.

Your Senior Cat's Social Life

As your cat grows older, her relationship with other members of your family may undergo some changes. How much and what kind of change, though, is unpredictable and will depend on a complicated set of factors, including your cat's individual personality and health.

Some older cats become reclusive, preferring to spend time by themselves and avoiding interaction part or most of the time. If this is your cat, she may be fine, but keep an eye on her, and if her urge for privacy comes on suddenly, have your vet check her out. Seeking solitude can be a sign of illness; cats are usually reluctant to show weakness.

Other cats become more mellow with age and more social than ever before. Your aging cat may want to spend a lot of time with people and other pets, particularly if she has a long-time relationship with one or more of them. Pets who have lived together for years often show obvious affection for

As your cat grows older, her relationship with family members and other pets may undergo some changes.

one another as they grow old together. Your cat also may go out of her way to show affection for one or more human family members. Many older cats become more vocal than they were when younger, so don't be surprised if your cat "talks" to you more than ever. She also may seek the company of her favorite people more often and be content to snuggle up for long periods.

Cats don't like change very much at any time in their lives, and as seniors, most felines become even less tolerant. The loss of a family member—like a grown child who leaves home or an older pet who dies—can be very

stressful for your cat. (See Chapter 6.) Similarly, the appearance of a new person or animal in the home may upset her. How quickly and how well she adjusts will depend on both your cat and the newcomer.

Many cats love children, but the sudden arrival of a baby or child in the house can be a shock. Don't put the entire burden of adjustment on your cat—that's not fair. Teach children to leave her alone unless she seeks their attention and to be gentle with her when she does. Supervise children who are too young to understand or comply. Be sure that your cat has a refuge where she can get away; if she is no longer able to jump up out of reach, you need to provide her with an option.

Other pets, too, can be a problem for your senior cat. If she has lived with the other animal for a while, they have probably worked out a reasonable relationship. A new pet, though, may frighten, hurt, or annoy your cat, especially if the newcomer is too pushy, playful, or big for your cat to fend off or escape. Kittens and puppies in particular can be too rough, and lacking the sense and restraint that come with maturity, a young animal may hurt an elderly cat without meaning to. (Of course, some animals do mean to hurt others, so be cautious when bringing a new pet into your home.) Be sure that your cat always has a way out, and

Senior cats experience many of the same problems that humans do, including loss of eyesight and hearing, arthritis, fatigue, dental problems, confusion, and so on.

supervise all interactions between the new pet and your feline until you are absolutely certain that they are okay together.

Should You Get a New Pet Now?

Does the potential for stress to your old cat mean that you shouldn't get another pet? That depends. Many people like to get another animal before the inevitable end of the old one's life. There's no question that having another pet at home can help when an old pet passes away, but it's important to balance your needs and desires against the needs and welfare of your geriatric cat.

The best time to bring a new pet home is while the older one is still in reasonably good health. If your senior feline is relatively healthy, mobile, and emotionally well adjusted, she will probably adjust to a new pet without too many problems. If, on the other hand, your older cat is ill or suffers from anxiety or other stress-related problems, this may not be the best time to add a new pet to your family.

If you do decide to bring home a new pet while your aging cat is still with you, you should be able to answer yes to all of these questions:

• Can I afford the cost of good geriatric veterinary care for my older cat as well as

The best time to bring a new pet home is while the older one is still in reasonably good health.

proper veterinary care for another pet? (Include routine and emergency care, and keep in mind that your aging cat could develop an age-related disease that requires treatment.)

- Can I afford all the other expenses of owning two pets? (Food, equipment, training for a dog, and so on.)
- Can I provide my older cat with a private refuge so that she can get away from the new pet?
- Can I manage the new pet well enough to protect my older cat from injury?
- Do I have time to spend with each animal individually every day to fulfill their emotional needs?
- Is my older cat well enough

physically and emotionally to handle the stress of a new pet in the house?

Adopting a Senior Cat

For reasons ranging from tragic to beyond senseless, many wonderful older adult cats become available for adoption through shelters and rescue organizations around the country. Unfortunately, they are often passed over in favor of kittens and younger adults, and the reason I hear most often is that "I won't have her very long." As someone who has adopted older animals, I have a few thoughts about that.

The cold, hard truth is that we never know how long we will have anyone.

Bringing Home an Older Cat

If you bring home an older cat, he may be afraid of his new surroundings and confused about where he is. Give him quiet time to explore and get comfortable. Don't invite friends and neighbors over to look at him, because this may make him nervous. Show the cat where the litter box, food and water dishes, and scratching post are, and then let him settle in at his own pace. Talk to him in a soothing voice, and give him something to eat. If he seems interested, play with him for a while so that he begins to bond with you.

An older cat has a history that you may not know about. He may have left a loving family or a long-time companion animal behind before he came to live with you, or he could have been mistreated or abandoned. If you happen to know the previous owners, or if you learned about his past when you adopted him, you can make settling in easier. If you know his name, use it often—it will give him a sense of comfort. If you don't, give your cat a chance to get used to his new one.

Some older cats will adapt to a new home right away, while others may hide under the bed for a day or two. Be patient, and give your feline companion plenty of love, praise, and encouragement while he makes the adjustment to living with you.

Some Like It Hot

In her latter years, our cat Mary spent hours, even in hot weather, curled up on a heating pad that we use for newborn puppies. If you want to provide a supplemental heat source for your cat, don't use a heating pad made for people—it could pose a fire or electrical hazard. Various types of heating pads designed for pets are available from pet supply stores.

Kittens die. Young adults die. And yes, old cats die too. But if we shy away because cats don't live forever and losing one is painful, we'd never have the pleasure of feline companionship at all.

An older adult cat in reasonably good health may be with you for more than a decade. She will be past the crazies of kittenhood. She is what she is—you can see whether she's a big cat or small, longhaired or shorthaired. You can tell a lot about her personality before you adopt her. She has the special dignity that comes to a cat who knows what life is about. And she needs you as much as you need her.

However your older cat came to be with you—as a kitten many years ago or as a senior adoptee —I hope that you have a journey ahead of many years together. I also hope that this book will help to make your journey smooth.

Chapter 2

The Well-Fed

Senior Cat

A healthful diet is fundamental to your senior cat's well-being and longevity. Good food supports her immune system, helping her to fend off infectious disease. Good food also helps to maintain the proper functioning of your cat's organs, her muscles and other supportive tissues, her sensory organs, and her mind. Poor food, in contrast, will do nothing to promote longevity and may contribute to a variety of health and behavior problems.

Choosing a good diet can be an intimidating process. A multitude of commercial cat foods fills the shelves of pet supply, grocery, and discount stores. There are foods for young cats, old cats, fit cats, fat cats, active cats, couch cats, sick cats, well cats—you name it. Or if you prefer to whip up a homemade diet for your cat, you can find recipes and diet plans galore in books, magazines, and on the Internet.

Yeow! How can you be sure that your cat's diet is healthful and the best that you can give her in her senior years? Knowledge, as they say, is power, so let's scratch out some facts about feline nutrition to help you decide.

Nutrients for a Balanced Feline Diet

Food is the nutritional fuel that powers your cat's internal engine. Food is made up of proteins, fats, carbohydrates, vitamins, minerals, other nutrients, and water, and for optimum health, these nutrients must come from high-quality sources and must be present in your cat's diet in specific proportions. Each nutrient supports specific bodily functions that contribute to physical and mental health.

Proteins

Proteins, made up of amino acids, are found in high concentrations in meat, fish, poultry, milk, cheese, yogurt, fish

meal, and eggs. Plants also contain proteins but lack certain amino acids found in meat sources. The protein content listed on a cat-food container indicates the total protein, but that can be misleading because the value of that protein to your cat depends on the quality of the ingredients and on the digestibility of the food.

Fats and Carbohydrates

Fats are found in meats, milk, butter, cheese, and vegetable oils. Dietary fat makes food taste better. More

Complete and Incomplete Proteins

Complete proteins, which are found in meats, fish, and eggs, provide all the amino acids that your cat needs to maintain good health. Incomplete proteins, in contrast, lack some amino acids that cats (and many other animals) require. Most plants provide incomplete proteins. Cats have much higher protein and fat requirements than do people, dogs, or many other mammals. As true carnivores, their diet should consist of about 30 percent protein. Cats also require taurine, an amino acid found in meat. Taurine deficiency causes blindness and can lead to fatal cardiomyopathy. Taurine occurs in trace amounts in some vegetables, but the amounts are too small to support feline health; this is why vegetarian diets are not suitable for cats.

cat's caloric needs remain pretty much the same throughout her life unless she becomes less active. If your cat loses weight or if her skin and fur become dry, ask your vet about a change in foods or about the addition of fatty acid supplements.

Carbohydrates ("carbs") are found in foods from plant sources. Carbohydrates provide energy. Although your cat is a carnivore with high protein needs, she does need some carbs in her diet as well.

Vitamins

Vitamins promote good health in a variety of ways. A high-quality feline diet provides vitamins in the proper amounts and in balance with one another. However, light, heat, moisture, and rancidity can easily destroy the chemicals that make up vitamins, thereby reducing the nutritional value of your cat's food. For that reason, it's essential to protect stored food from heat, light, and moisture, and to use it before its expiration date. As important as they are, though, more is not better when it comes to vitamins; in fact, an excess of some vitamins can make your cat ill. Too much vitamin A, for instance, can damage her bones.

Minerals

Minerals are vital to strong bones, healthy cell tissue, and properly

A healthy, nutritionally balanced diet is fundamental to your senior cat's well-being and longevity.

importantly, fat provides energy, protects internal organs, insulates against cold, and transports vitamins and other nutrients within the body.

Although fat tends to get a bad rap, it is vital to good health. In fact, studies have shown that as cats age, they lose their ability to digest and absorb dietary fat, and as a result, they need to eat fat that is more easily digested to maintain their weight and energy. And unlike dogs (and people!), who need fewer calories as they get older, your

Supplements Caution

Dietary supplements may seem like a good way to ensure your cat's proper nutrition, and some supplements are good for some cats. However, excess vitamins and minerals in the diet can cause serious problems. If you feed a high-quality cat food, supplements should not be necessary. Ask your vet before adding supplements to your cat's diet.

functioning organs. High-quality feline diets provide minerals in the proper balance. As with vitamins, though, too much of some minerals can cause serious health problems, including kidney stones and skeletal problems.

Water

Water is an essential part of your cat's diet. It keeps her body properly hydrated and helps her organs function. Senior cats are particularly subject to dehydration, so you must make it easy for her to take in enough water every day, particularly if she eats dry

food. Your cat gets some of her water indirectly from her food and some directly by drinking. She should always have easy access to clean water. If her mobility becomes limited as she ages, help her by placing water bowls in all parts of the house that she frequents.

Basic Feline Nutrition

The nutritional value of any particular food is different for different species and individuals, depending on the animal's nutritional requirements and the ability of the animal's digestive system to utilize the nutrients in that food. No matter how sweet and cuddly your cat may be, she is much like her cousin the tiger. Her teeth are perfectly designed to grasp prey and to shear off hunks of meat, but they are not very

Older cats are particularly subject to dehydration, so make it easy for your senior to take in enough water by placing water bowls in all parts of the house.

good at chewing up vegetable matter. Her digestive tract processes meat proteins efficiently but cannot break down the tough cellulose walls of vegetable matter as can grazing and browsing animals. In short, your cat is a carnivore—a meat eater.

Does that mean that she doesn't need vegetables? No, not at all. But she needs her veggies "broken down" for her so that her digestive system can make use of their nutrients. In the wild, cats eat the stomachs and intestines of their prey, including the partially digested contents. Your domestic cat needs the bulk of her vegetable matter cooked. She also may enjoy fresh greens, although their nutritional value is minimal.

Knowing the basic principles of feline nutrition is a helpful step toward keeping your cat healthy throughout her life. Remember, though, that your cat is an individual, and her needs may be slightly different from those of another cat. The best clues to how well your cat's diet suits her are her health and physical appearance. You can expect some changes to occur to her body as she ages (see Chapter 6), but she should have a reasonable layer of flesh between her skin and her bones. Her skin and coat should appear to be healthy, and although she may sleep more as she ages, when she's awake she should be reasonably active; if not, ask your veterinarian whether a change in diet might help.

Commerical Cat Foods

Commercial cat foods offer a major benefit for today's busy cat owner: convenience. The good foods also offer high-quality ingredients combined into carefully balanced blends that have benefited from many years of extensive scientific research and feedback from cat owners and veterinarians.

Stroll through the cat food aisles in your local pet supply store and you'll find a stunning variety of products available. You will find foods based on fish, chicken, turkey, beef, lamb, duck,

Greens for Your Cat

Some cats enjoy fresh greens. The following "cat greens" are easy to grow if you're so inclined. (Warning: Avoid seeds treated with herbicides or insecticides.)

- grass (bluegrass, fescue, ryegrass)
- Japanese barnyard millet
- oats
- rye (but beware of ergot, a hallucinogenic fungus)
- sprouts (alfalfa or bean), in small amounts
- wheat

Knowing the basic principles of proper feline nutrition is a helpful step toward keeping your cat healthy throughout her life.

venison, eggs, or a combination. You can choose dry foods, semi-moist foods, canned foods, or frozen foods. There are formulas for kittens, adults, and seniors, as well as for lazy cats and active cats. Does your cat have a specific problem? You can find a food to combat tartar, alleviate allergies, calm the kidneys, handle hairballs, and take off excess weight—name a concern, and there's probably a food that's supposed to help.

Unfortunately, those obvious differences aren't the only ones you need to consider. Cat foods are definitely not all created equal in quality. Your cat can't shop for herself, so it's important to know what you're buying for her sake.

Although cats are not the most expensive of pets to feed, the cost can add up, and it's sometimes tempting to cut corners on food choices. But very cheap food is false economy in the long run because a long-term diet of poor-quality food often leads to health problems that require expensive veterinary care.

Lower-quality foods include fillers with little or no nutritional value. They also use lower-quality proteins and often include food dyes and preservatives that have been linked to allergies and other health problems. The ingredients in cheaper foods are often less digestible, meaning more and smellier feces—a big consideration if you're the one who cleans the litter box! Cats on poor diets are more prone to vomiting, and the dyes in some lower-quality foods stain everything they touch. Those dyes are there to make you think that

How to Change Your Senior Cat's Food

Age often makes the digestive system more intolerant of change, and a sudden switch to a new food may cause vomiting and/or diarrhea. If you need to change your senior cat's food, make the change gradually, slowly increasing the proportion of new food and decreasing the old over the course of a week or two.

the food looks better, by the way—your cat doesn't care what color her food is as long as it smells good and fills her tummy.

Allergies and other sensitivities can develop through exposure, so as your cat ages, she may no longer tolerate dyes and food additives that didn't bother her when she was younger. In other words, even if she has eaten a particular food for years with no problems, there may come a time when she can no longer eat that food. If you notice changes in your cat's skin and coat, elimination patterns, or behavior, or if she develops bad breath or gains or loses weight, talk to your vet, and keep in mind that many health problems are food related.

High-quality foods do cost a bit more per bag (or can) because they contain better ingredients. On the other hand, they are nutritionally denser and are more easily digested than poorer foods, so your cat can eat less food per meal and get better nutrition. The cost per meal may be about the same, and the health benefits of better food are incalculable.

Price alone does not indicate high quality, of course. Some of the more expensive cat foods offer more in advertisements that tug at your heart than they offer in food quality. I'd suggest that you spend some time reading labels in a pet supply store and perusing some of the websites recommended in this chapter so that you can make an informed decision about the best food for your aging cat.

Now let's take a look at some of your other commercial cat food options.

High-quality cat foods are recommended for seniors because they are nutritionally denser and more easily digested than poorer foods.

Dry Foods

Dry food, or "kibble," offers a number of advantages. It is easy to feed and store, and it doesn't get messy. Dry food is readily available in a wide range of qualities, prices, and ingredients. It tends to keep your cat's teeth cleaner because particles are less likely to stick to her teeth and gums, and the hard bits tend to scrape the teeth clean as she chews. Dry food also makes for firmer, less-fragrant stools. It tends to cost less than moist and wet foods of equal quality, and it keeps longer and has a milder odor.

There are, however, potential drawbacks to dry food. First, as your cat gets older, she may find it difficult to chew. Second, a cat on dry food needs to drink more water. Normally that shouldn't be a problem, but if your older cat has trouble getting around, it's essential that you make it easy for her to get to her water bowl. Finally, the low odor level of dry food may make it less interesting to your cat as her senses become duller with age. However, if you put a little warm water or salt-free broth on it to make it more fragrant, her interest will likely increase.

Semi-Moist Foods

Semi-moist foods, which typically come in packets, are essentially soft kibble. These foods are commonly more expensive than kibble. They usually contain dyes to make them more

Learn More About Cat Foods

Visit www.petfoodreport.com to learn more about cat foods. This website is designed to help pet owners sort through all the information available about commercial pet foods, as well as addressing frequently asked questions. It also assists pet owners in understanding food labels and provides additional information on ingredients, proper nutrition, and feeding guidelines.

visually appealing to cat owners, and they almost invariably contain chemical preservatives. Both dyes and preservatives have been linked to a number of health problems, including allergies and hyperactivity. Semi-moist foods also tend to stick to the teeth and gums, promoting the development of tartar, and eventually, gum disease. This type of food should not be the sole source of nutrition available to your cat.

Canned Foods

Canned, or wet, foods are more expensive than dry foods of equal quality. (You pay for the can and the added cost of shipping the water in the food.) For cats with certain medical conditions, including many senior cats, a good canned food is the best dietary choice. On the other hand, a diet of just

quality proteins, excess fats, preservatives, dyes, and other chemicals, all of which have been linked to serious health and behavior problems. Be a smart consumer—you and your cat will both be better off.

Homemade Cat Foods

Some cat owners prefer to prepare the meals they serve their feline friends. If you have time to research, plan, shop, and prepare the food, as well as room to store the ingredients, you may prefer to make your cat's food yourself.

Some homemade diets include cooked meats, vegetables, fruits, and grains. Others focus on raw ingredients, including meaty chicken and turkey bones, organ meat (liver, kidney, heart, brain, tongue, and tripe), and eggs. You can add green leafy vegetables after running them through a food processor or juicer to break down the cellulose. Some people also add one or more of the following: vegetable oils, brewer's yeast, kelp, apple cider vinegar, fruits, raw honey, dairy products (particularly raw goat milk, cottage cheese, and plain yogurt), and small helpings of grain.

The major attraction to homemade diets, whether raw or cooked, is that you know what your cat is eating because you select and prepare the ingredients. Of course, having to select ingredients and prepare your cat's food is also a drawback because of the time required to shop, make the food, and clean up.

Treats

If you're like most cat owners, you probably like to give your cat special treats once in a while. In reasonable amounts, treats are fine, but remember that they add to your cat's daily calories. Treats also may contain food dyes, preservatives, and other chemicals. So follow the same basic guidelines as for foods—find nutritionally balanced treats, avoid dyes and other chemicals, and don't overdo it.

canned food can cause flatulence, bad breath, and soft, strong-smelling stools. If your cat needs to eat canned food, pay special attention to her dental care to prevent tartar from building up and causing gum disease. (See Chapter 4.)

Cleanliness, which is always important, is critical if you feed canned cat food because it spoils quickly and attracts insects and rodents.

A good commercial cat food will provide your cat with properly balanced nutrition, promoting her good health and longevity. Poor-quality commercial cat foods, though, contain questionable ingredients, including low-

No Cooked Bones

Cooked bones can kill your cat. They splinter when they break, and the sharp ends can perforate her esophagus, stomach, or intestines. Your vet sometimes may be able to repair the damage surgically, but not always. So don't feed your cat cooked bones, and be sure that garbage is kept safely out of reach.

Proper handling of ingredients, especially meats, is an essential part of preparing homemade pet food. Raw meat and poultry contain bacteria that can cause food poisoning and may also harbor parasites and their eggs and larvae. These unwelcome critters may endanger not only your cat and other pets, but also you and your human family, so utensils, containers, and work spaces must be kept scrupulously clean. Many people wear plastic gloves when handling raw meat. Whether or not you do, always wash your hands thoroughly with soap and water afterward.

Unlike a pet-food manufacturer, you don't have a full-time staff of nutritionists and researchers at your disposal, so if you feed your cat a homemade diet, you will have to spend time learning as much as possible about feline nutrition to ensure that you provide all the nutrients your cat needs. She doesn't have to eat a fully balanced diet every day, but over several days she needs to take in the proper balance of proteins, carbohydrates, fats, minerals, and vitamins. If not, all your work will be in vain.

A complete discussion of nutritious homemade cat foods is beyond the scope of this book, but you

Scheduled feeding works best with seniors; with an older cat, it's especially important to know that she's eating properly.

Obesity and Feline Life Expectancy

Despite the supposedly humorous photos we see of fat cats, excess weight is no laughing matter. Studies show that obesity is hard on the heart, lungs, pancreas, kidneys, joints, and muscles, and it can lower your cat's life expectancy by 30 to 50 percent.

can find accurate information at your library or on the Internet. Be careful, though—a lot of people post bad information on websites and discussion lists. Check the writer's credentials, and don't rely on a single source. Also, work with your veterinarian, especially if your aging cat is being treated for any health problems.

Free Feeding Versus Scheduled Feeding

Many people prefer to make dry food available so that their cats can eat whenever they want to. Such free feeding works well for many cats and cat owners. For others, scheduled meals are more conducive to good health.

For one thing, some cats overeat when given an "all you can eat" buffet. Garfield isn't the only fat cat around! If you have more than one cat, feeding individual portions on a schedule will enable you to notice if one of them stops eating—often the first sign of illness or injury. With your older cat, it's especially important to know that she's eating properly. If your cats eat different foods, scheduled meals are the only way to control who gets what.

If your cat is used to being free fed, she may not be amused if you switch to scheduled meals. But no matter what she may think, you are in charge, and she will adjust to eating on schedule in a few days.

The night before the first day of the new feeding schedule, pick up your cat's food (leave the water.) The next day at mealtime, put the food down for about half an hour. If your cat is used to snacking as she pleases all day, she may be hungry and gobble her food. Or she may turn up her nose and walk away, thinking that you made a mistake that has now been corrected. Whether she eats or not, pick up the food after half an hour (unless she's actively eating). Don't give her any more to eat until the next mealtime. If you have more than one cat, separate them during meals, or supervise so that everyone gets their fair share. An elderly cat in particular may eat more slowly and have trouble keeping another cat from taking her food.

It may take your cat a day or two to catch on, but she will. Scheduled meals will soon be a normal part of daily life.

Fat Cats

Most of us know by now that excess weight contributes to many serious health problems and shortens life spans. That's as true for cats as it is for people. Very rarely, obesity is due, at least in part, to a medical problem. More often, though, excess weight is the direct result of an animal eating more calories than she burns.

Several factors determine how much food your cat needs to maintain a proper weight and optimum health:

- **Activity Level:** An active cat needs more food than a couch kitty. As long as your cat remains active, her caloric needs will remain about the same.
- **Quality of Food:** The nutritional value and calories in commercial and homemade feline diets vary widely.

As your cat ages, she may need fewer calories per day to maintain her weight if she becomes less active.

A Sense of Smell

Your nose has about 5 million odor-sensing cells. Your cat's nose is about 40 times as well equipped, having about 200 million of the odor-sensing cells!

The higher the nutritional value of your cat's food, the less she needs to eat.

- **Individual Variations:** Your cat is an individual, with her own looks, personality, and nutritional needs.

If your cat has packed on some extra weight, it's up to you to help her slim down. If you've been free feeding, switch to scheduled meals so that you can control what she eats. Be aware that the portions recommended on most commercial cat foods are estimates and may be too much for your cat, especially if her energy expenditures have slowed down. Use manufacturer

Special foods are available that are designed to help aging cats with a wide variety of health challenges.

recommendations as a starting point, and then adjust your cat's daily rations according to her weight. A weight-reduction food may help, but I've seen many overweight pets who have eaten "weight-control" formulas for years. The simple fact is that too much food leads to excess weight.

Finicky Eaters

Your cat has the same sensory organs that you do: eyes, ears, nose, taste buds, and the organs of touch. But her senses work differently than yours do, and a normal, healthy cat has a better sense of smell than you have. In fact, she lives in a much richer world of scent and uses scents to communicate with other cats, to sense danger, to navigate, and to locate prey. Certain smells undoubtedly give her pleasure as well.

Got Cream?

Want to give your old friend an occasional dairy treat? Make it cream. Most adult cats are lactose intolerant, and milk gives them diarrhea. Cream, on the other hand, contains less lactose, and most cats tolerate it. Cats also like the high-butterfat taste of cream, but too much of that milk fat will turn to cat fat. If your cat has any health problems, consult your vet. If she says that cream is okay, keep servings small and infrequent.

As she ages, your cat may lose some of her ability to sense smells, and food may lose some of its appeal. If she becomes finicky about her food as she advances in age, you may be able to revive her appetite by increasing her food's fragrance. You can do this by adding warm water or salt-free broth to dry food or by warming wet food slightly. (But don't make the water or broth too hot!)

Special Diets

Cats with certain medical conditions often benefit from specific dietary changes. Specially designed foods are available that are designed to help cats with a wide variety of health challenges, and your vet may recommend such a food at some point in your feline's life.

On the other hand, you are much better equipped than your cat is to distinguish different flavors. The average person has some 9,000 taste buds on the tip, sides, and back of the tongue—18 times as many as the paltry 475 on your cat's tongue. So fragrance plays a much more important role than taste in stimulating your cat's appetite.

Throughout your cat's life, a good-quality food is one of the best investments you can make in her health and well-being. Your cat is indeed, at least in part, what she eats.

Chapter 3

The Well-Groomed

Senior Cat

Cats have a well-deserved reputation for cleanliness, and most keep themselves as clean and tidy as possible. Still, regular grooming is an essential part of caring for a cat, and it becomes even more important as your cat's years add up. Old joints become stiff and sore, the senses lose their sharpness, and energy wanes, making it difficult for your old friend to groom herself.

A small investment of your time will keep your cat (and your house) cleaner and healthier and provide a regular opportunity for you to examine her for lumps, bumps, fleas, and other signs of illness or injury. Grooming sessions also will reinforce the bond between you and your feline companion.

Coat and Skin Care

Advancing age will bring changes in your cat's skin and fur. She may show gray or white hair, especially on her face (unless she's white). Her fur also may become thinner, and its texture may change as well. Her skin may lose

Proper grooming is important throughout your cat's life but especially so in her senior years.

its elasticity and become thinner, dryer, more fragile, and slower to heal. (Such changes also can be signs of health problems or nutritional deficiencies, so consult your veterinarian if your cat's coat changes suddenly or significantly.) Healthy skin and coat begin with proper nutrition, health care, and parasite control, but regular brushing and perhaps an occasional bath help too.

Brushing

Brushing stimulates the sebaceous (oil) glands in your cat's skin and distributes the oils to lubricate the skin and coat. If your cat has long hair, brushing is

Teach Your Old Cat to Love Being Groomed

If your senior feline isn't used to being brushed, begin slowly. Brush her a little, and then pet her. Talk softly to reassure her. Most cats enjoy being brushed on the tops of their necks and their heads, so start there and slowly move to other areas. You can groom your cat on your lap, or put her on a table covered with a towel or rubber mat for traction.

essential to remove tangles and prevent mats from forming. Brushing also will remove a lot of hair that would otherwise fall on your floors, furniture, and clothes, or turn into hairballs in your cat's stomach.

Keep in mind that old skin is delicate. Don't pull too hard on your cat's hair or press too hard against her skin with the brush or comb. Brushing a dry coat can break hair and create static electricity, so it's best to add some moisture. If your cat will let you, very lightly spritz her fur with water from a spray bottle before brushing. Most cats object to such rude behavior, though. If yours does, spray her brush lightly instead. Begin brushing at the front of your cat's body. Pick up small sections of hair at skin level and brush them forward, toward your cat's head. Work your way back on one side, brushing small sections forward until you reach the tail. Then brush the sections of hair back in the right direction, beginning at the rear and working forward to the head. Then brush the other side. Do the same with the tail, starting at the base and moving to the tip. Brush your cat's

As your cat ages, stiffening joints and waning energy may make it difficult for your old friend to groom herself.

Grooming as a Health Check

Grooming sessions are the perfect time to check your cat for potential health problems. After all, the sooner you catch a problem, the better chance that your veterinarian has to fix it. So while grooming, look for the following:

- lumps, sores, or tender areas anywhere on her body or changes in her fur or skin
- excess discharge from her eyes, signs of squinting, or other abnormal eye appearance
- excess discharge from her nose
- excess discharge or sore or red areas in her ears
- cuts or other abnormalities on her feet
- redness or sores on her gums, loose teeth, lumps in the mouth, or drooling

chest beginning high on the neck and brushing small sections upward, then smoothing them back in the right direction, working from the bottom

up. When your cat is comfortable being brushed, do her belly the same way.

If your cat has long fur, it's important to remove any mats that form because matted fur holds moisture and skin oil, which can cause skin inflammations and harbor parasites. Unfortunately, mats can be difficult to remove without injuring the skin. If you are hesitant about removing them, take your cat to a good groomer who is experienced handling cats. Once the mats have been removed, prevent new ones with regular brushing.

Bathing

Yes, cats can be bathed, and cat bathers can survive the process. Most felines don't need to be bathed very often, but occasionally a bath is necessary. If someone in your household has allergies, regular rinsing or bathing can remove allergens from the fur. If your cat is exposed to a toxic substance such as a garden chemical or household cleaner, a bath will remove the poisons that she would otherwise ingest by licking. If she

Grooming Supplies for Different Coat Types

As with any job, the right tools make cat grooming a lot easier. For long, thick fur, use a pin brush, which has straight metal pins 1 inch (2.5 cm) or so long. A soft bristle brush works well on long, silky fur. To remove loose hairs from short fur, use a rubber brush. A metal or Teflon-coated comb is good for a final touch, especially on long coats. If you think that your cat has fleas, a flea comb with small teeth set close together to trap the insects is useful.

Advancing age will bring changes in your cat's skin and fur. Brushing will improve circulation and keep her fur smooth and shiny.

gets fleas, you can remove them by bathing as part of a comprehensive flea-control program. Here's how to give your cat a bath and live to tell about it.

First, brush your cat thoroughly, particularly if she has a long coat. You must remove all tangles and mats, because once they get wet, they will be almost impossible to comb out, and if left after the bath, they will hold moisture, creating a perfect place for bacteria and yeast to reproduce. For your own protection, you may want to trim your cat's claws, too.

Choose a mild shampoo formulated for cats, and use it sparingly and according to directions. Some pet shampoos need to be diluted, and even those that don't are easier to apply and to rinse out if diluted with an equal part water.

You can find all sorts of special cat shampoos, although for most purposes you don't need anything fancy. No-rinse shampoos can be handy because you don't need to wet or rinse your cat with water. If you don't want to get her wet at all, a dry cat shampoo can be used to clean mildly oily skin. If your cat gets a petroleum product on her fur, use a mild dish detergent;

Don't Be Shocked

veterinarians recommend Dawn to remove oil. (Rescuers often use Dawn to clean up victims of oil spills.) The detergent also will remove skin oils, though, so use a moisturizing conditioner on your cat afterward. Do not use flea shampoos or medicated shampoos without consulting your vet, especially if your cat has any kind of medical condition. The chemicals in such products can be harsh, and some will interact with medications. In addition, avoid perfumed shampoos and other products. What smells nice to you may be overpowering to your cat.

Before you start, gather the following supplies:

- pet shampoo
- one or two towels
- gentle sprayer or unbreakable container for rinsing
- towel, mat, or screen for the bottom of the tub

Unless your cat is very large, the kitchen sink is a good "cat tub." She will not like the slippery wet floor of the sink, so give her better traction by placing a towel or bath mat on the bottom. If she is difficult to control, you might want to invest in a "bath sack" that envelopes the body up to the

The Expert Knows

Preventing Hairballs

The infamous hairball is formed when your cat ingests hair while licking herself. Her stomach cannot digest the hairs, and they glom together into a ball. As owners know all too well, most cats cough up their hairballs. Sometimes, though, hairballs cause vomiting, constipation, and loss of appetite, and in severe cases they must be surgically removed. You can protect your cat from these problems by brushing her frequently, especially when she's shedding, and by feeding food designed to prevent hairballs. If the problem is frequent or severe, talk to your vet.

> *Most cats don't need to be bathed often, but if a bath is necessary, talk to your senior in a soothing voice to help her remain calm.*

Put your cat in the sink, grip her scruff firmly, and wet her with warm (not hot) water, being careful not to get any in her ears. Apply a small amount of shampoo, and work it gently through her fur, avoiding her ears and eyes. Rinse her completely, paying special attention to the spots where soap hides—the belly, groin, and armpits. Gently squeeze as much water as you can from her fur, and then wrap her in a towel. Being wrapped up calms most cats, so hold her, talk to her, and let the towel absorb as much water as possible. When your cat begins to relax, keep a firm grip on her, remove the wet towel, and replace it with a dry one. The more water you can remove from her fur, the less likely she is to catch a chill.

Keep your cat in a warm, draft-free place until she's completely dry. If she has long hair, brush or comb through it while it's still damp. If your cat will

neck, allowing you to bathe her through the sack while maintaining control. They are available from many pet supply stores.

A gentle spray attachment will make wetting and rinsing your cat easier. If you don't have a sprayer, a pressurized garden sprayer (the ordinary hand-pumped type) will work. Just be sure that it has never been used for toxic chemicals. You can also simply pour rinse water over your cat using an unbreakable container.

An aging cat may have trouble keeping her claws trimmed, so regular nail care will help to keep her feet healthy.

tolerate it, you can dry her further with a hair dryer set on low or cool (never hot).

Nail Care

Your cat's claws, like your nails, grow constantly (unless she has been declawed). Newly grown claws are protected by an outer layer that the cat removes by "sharpening" them, preferably on a scratching post. As your cat grows older, though, she may become unable to maintain her own pedicures. Her claws also may become dryer and more brittle as she ages, making them more prone to splitting and catching on carpets, upholstery, and clothing.

You can help to keep your cat's claws and feet healthy by trimming her claws on a regular basis. Even if you didn't trim them when she was younger, she can learn that getting a trim is no big deal.

The first step is to get your cat used to having her paws handled. Don't try to trim her claws at first. Begin by casually holding and massaging each of the paws whenever she's sitting quietly on your lap. Put your index finger on the toe pad and your thumb on top of the paw, and gently press until the claw extends from the sheath. Don't squeeze too hard.

When your cat is comfortable having her feet handled, begin

trimming. You can purchase a claw clipper made for cats, although I've always used a standard nail clipper made for people. If your cat won't hold still while you trim, wrap her snugly in a towel, freeing only the paw you are trimming. Extend the claws as you did before, and trim the ones on the front feet, including the dew claws (the small claws on the front legs

FAMILY-FRIENDLY TIP
Kiddie Cat Grooming

Your child can learn a lot about responsible pet care and the importance of personal hygiene by helping to keep your cat well groomed. Which grooming tasks your child can take on will depend on your child's age and ability, and on your cat's condition, personality, and attitude toward being groomed. If she enjoys being brushed, that's a good job for a child to begin with, although an adult may need to hold the cat throughout the process. Leave more delicate tasks such as ear and teeth cleaning and claw clipping to an adult or to an older child under adult supervision. In fact, an adult should supervise all grooming to be sure that it is gentle and thorough and to end the session if the cat shows signs of stress.

No Ear Swabs, Please!

Never insert anything, including cotton swabs, into your cat's ears. You could impact any wax that is present and cause other serious injuries.

above the feet). Rear claws don't need to be trimmed as often, if ever—they aren't as sharp as the front ones, and they grow more slowly.

The tip of the claw has no nerves, so trimming it does not hurt. The live center of the claw is a different story. Called the quick, it contains nerves and blood, so if you cut into it, your cat will experience pain and the claw will bleed. Luckily for both of you, most cat claws lack pigment, and the quick appears darker, or sometimes pinker, than the rest of the claw, so it's easy to see.

Because only the sharp tip of the claw needs to be trimmed, you shouldn't find avoiding the quick too difficult. If you do accidentally cut the claw too short and cause bleeding, stop it by dipping it in styptic powder (available from veterinarians, pet supply stores, or the shaving section of many other stores) or cornstarch. (If the claw continues to bleed for longer than ten minutes, or if the blood is spurting, call your vet.)

With regular trimming, your older cat's claws and paws will stay healthier, even if she can no longer take care of

To check the inner part of your cat's ear, hold the tip between your thumb and forefinger and roll it gently toward the back of her head. The skin should be pink or flesh colored and should look healthy and clean, with no red or sore-looking patches. A little bit of light brown wax is normal, but heavy discharge (especially black, red, or green-yellow) indicates a problem. If the ears look healthy and your cat shows no signs of discomfort around her ears or head, gently wipe away any excess wax with a pad soaked in ear cleanser.

Ear problems are hard to diagnose, and treating for the wrong type of infection won't help and might make things worse, so if your cat's ears look red, sore, or dirty, or if she scratches her ears or shakes her head a lot, see your vet.

Older cats often lose some or all of their hearing, but hearing loss isn't always easy for us to detect. If your cat doesn't react to sounds that used to attract or startle her, chances are she's hard of hearing. This is not usually a

Bad Breath

Your cat should not have chronically bad breath. If she does, here are some possible causes:

- **Diet:** Some foods, especially soft foods, leave particles on the teeth and gums and attract bacteria that cause bad breath. A change of food may help. If it doesn't, talk to your vet.
- **Gum Disease:** Red, puffy gums in an adult cat indicate disease or infection. See your vet.
- **Abscesses:** Your cat may hide the pain, but an infected or abscessed tooth requires veterinary attention to prevent serious complications.
- **Illness:** Problems farther down the digestive tract may cause bad breath. See your vet.

them herself. She also will be less likely to snag your carpets, upholstery, and clothes.

Ear Care

Good ear care is important to your cat's health, especially as she ages. Check her ears at least once a week, and clean them as needed to prevent ear mites, allergies, and bacterial, fungal, and yeast infections from taking hold.

Common Signs of Dental Disease

Symptoms of dental disease include:

- bad breath
- difficulty eating or drinking
- drooling
- unexplained weight loss

problem for a house cat, but without the ability to hear, she is vulnerable to serious injury outdoors. Indoor cats lead longer, healthier lives, and keeping your senior cat indoors may extend her life by many years.

Dental Care

Good dental care is important throughout your cat's life and especially so in her senior years. Broken or loose teeth, gum disease, abscesses, or decay can all cause pain and may contribute to health and behavior problems. Cats are reluctant to show their pain, and oral problems may be well advanced and very painful before you realize that your cat has a problem.

Periodontal (gum) disease is very common in cats. From the time your senior feline started eating solid food many years ago, bacteria and food particles have accumulated along her gum line and under her gums, forming plaque. If it is not removed, plaque soon hardens into calculus, which irritates the gums and eventually causes serious problems, including tooth and bone loss and infection. Bacteria from unhealthy gums can enter the bloodstream and damage the heart, kidneys, and other internal organs. Fortunately, a program of preventive dental care can keep your cat's mouth healthy, prolong her life, and improve its quality. If she

43

has not been on a dental care regime, ask your vet for advice on getting started. It's never too late to begin.

Daily brushing is ideal, but realistically, brushing your cat's teeth even two or three times a week will keep her teeth and gums healthier. In addition, you'll notice signs of oral problems, including foul breath, loose or missing teeth, sores, lumps, and so on that may need veterinary attention.

Special toothbrushes, "finger" brushes, and tooth-cleaning pads are available for use on cats, or you can use a small child's toothbrush with soft bristles. Don't use human toothpaste or baking soda—they can pose health risks if swallowed, and most cats don't like the taste.

Purchase toothpaste made for cats from your vet or a pet supply store.

Begin with very short sessions, and don't try to brush at first. Put some kitty toothpaste on your finger and run it briefly along your cat's teeth and gums. Pet and praise her. Increase the amount of time that you spend each session until you can rub the outer surfaces of all your cat's teeth and gums. (Cats seldom develop periodontal problems on the inner edges of the teeth because their raspy tongues clean those surfaces.) Then it's time to introduce the brush. Be patient and keep tooth-cleaning sessions short. Cuddle or play with your cat afterward.

Your senior cat will be healthier and happier if you help her with the personal care she can no longer manage.

Finding a Professional Pet Groomer

Some owners may find it challenging to safely and properly groom an older pet. When your cat needs grooming in her senior years, great patience and skill are necessary to ensure that she is comfortable and secure. For this reason, many owners may prefer to pay a professional pet groomer to tend to their aging cat's grooming needs. One way to find a reputable groomer is to ask friends, relatives, and coworkers who own cats to recommend someone. If possible, find a "cats-only" groomer. He will have lots of experience dealing with cats, and your feline won't be frightened or distracted by the scents and sounds of dogs or other animals in the establishment.

Choose a groomer who is friendly, patient, and who takes the time to explain her services to you. Make sure that he has experience dealing with older animals. Ask to tour the facility (make sure it's clean), and see if the groomer will let you watch her groom someone else's cat to see how he interacts with and handles the animal. Get references from all the groomers you visit and check them.

When you find a groomer whom you'd like to use, bring your cat in for a first-time visit. Sit with her while the groomer is working, and watch how the process is done. Talk to your senior in a soothing voice if she becomes scared or nervous. If your cat becomes very upset, you may want to consider trying to groom her at home yourself or perhaps your vet can refer you to an at-home grooming service.

In addition to home dental care, your cat should have an oral examination along with her annual physical, and your vet may recommend more frequent exams and other procedures. Most cats seven years old and older should have dental exams every six months. Your vet also may recommend full-mouth or partial X-rays to identify problems under the gum line, and your cat may need periodic professional cleanings under anesthesia. Although anesthesia poses some risks, new short-acting injectable anesthetics are much safer than older anesthetics. Ask your vet what kind of anesthesia he uses, how easy it is to reverse, and how your cat will be monitored while under it.

Grooming as Bonding Time

Grooming your older cat regularly requires a little effort, but the benefits are more than just good looks. Your cat will be healthier, and she'll be happy to have you help her with the personal care she can no longer manage herself. Best of all, you'll share special time together, and you will both be happier for it.

Chapter 4

Routine Health Care

Good health care, including daily attention at home and visits to the veterinarian, is essential if you want your cat to stay healthy as long as possible. Even if she seems to be fine, regular veterinary care can detect potential problems, and ideally, keep them under control. Many veterinarians now offer geriatric preventive care programs designed to prolong the lives and good health of older animals. In addition to the regular general examinations recommended throughout life, geriatric wellness programs usually include additional diagnostic tests as appropriate for the individual cat.

Among the tests that may be included at different intervals are urinalysis, blood count (CBC), blood chemistry panel, testing for FIV and FeLV, electrocardiogram (EKG), thyroid testing, radiographs (X-rays), blood pressure monitoring, and pre-anesthetic screening if your cat needs anesthesia.

You also play an important part in your cat's wellness program, of course. Hopefully, you handle your cat every day. When you cuddle or groom her, pay attention to anything different or unusual you may notice, and tell your vet about any lumps, sores, hair loss, changes in eating or elimination habits, sudden weight gain or loss, strange odors, or other physical changes. Watch her behavior as well—health problems can be at the root of behavioral changes. You can expect some changes as your cat gets older, but extreme or sudden changes may be symptomatic of illness or disease.

Although not the most pleasant part of owning a cat, the fact is that the litter box can provide clues to your cat's health. Changes in the amount or color of her urine, or in the color, consistency, volume, and frequency of her bowel movements, may signal health issues. Similarly, although older cats typically lose some weight as they lose muscle, a sudden gain or loss of more than a pound or two (0.5 to 1 kg) may be significant. Tell your veterinarian about any of these changes.

Veterinary Senior Care

Veterinary medicine has come a long way over the past few decades. Many new procedures are available for testing and treating pets, including ultrasound, laser surgery, electrosurgery, and endoscopy. These

FAMILY-FRIENDLY TIP

Good Health Is a Family Affair

If there is a positive side to our pets' short lives, it is that they teach us about the life cycle. For many children these days, an aging pet is the "oldest" being they know, and perhaps a child's only contact with "the elderly." If your cat has health problems, even minor ones, be sure that your child understands that kitty doesn't feel well, or is sore, or can't hear or see. How much you explain will, naturally, depend on your child's age, but even young kids need to learn to respect the kitty's need for rest and privacy. As aging leads to more profound changes in your cat's health and behavior, teach your child to be extra patient and gentle. Be sure that your cat has a private place to rest undisturbed, especially if her mobility is limited, and supervise all interaction between your cat and child.

new methods are often excellent choices for older cats because they take less time and are less invasive than their predecessors, or they require local rather than general anesthesia. As we shall see later in this chapter, holistic and alternative approaches to veterinary medicine also have become more popular.

Another aspect of animal health care that has improved a lot in recent years is pain control. In the past, chronic or post-surgical pain was usually treated conservatively or ignored altogether, leaving cats to suffer in silence. Although many pain relievers cannot be used for cats, new pain-relief medications have been developed that are safe and effective, especially for elderly cats.

Some changes that come with the years affect your cat's ability to handle her environment. She will be less able to regulate her body temperature than when she was younger, and changes in her internal temperature can damage her heart and lungs. Her hearing and vision will become less acute, and her reaction time slower, putting her more at risk of accidents or of being attacked by other animals. She also may become disoriented at times and could become lost. If your cat has been used to going outdoors, you may not want to confine her all the time. Nevertheless, there's no question that cats live longer, healthier lives indoors. At the least, consider limiting the time your older

Good health care, daily attention, and regular vet visits are essential if you want your senior cat to stay healthy as long as possible.

cat spends outdoors, especially at night or when the temperature is very hot or cold.

The Right Veterinarian

If you have had your cat for many years, chances are you have a long-standing relationship with your veterinarian. Still, there are times when it becomes necessary to find a new vet—if you move, for instance, or if your vet retires. You also may decide to change your cat's doctor for other reasons. Here are some suggestions to help you choose the best vet for your needs and your cat's health.

First, decide what's important to you. Do you want to be there when the vet examines your cat, or do you prefer to drop her off and pick her up later? Do you need evening or Saturday appointments? Are you comfortable with the clinic's emergency services? Does its payment and billing policies meet your needs? Recommendations from friends are useful for narrowing down your choices. On the other hand, your cousin's favorite vet may not suit you, so try to interview those who interest you before your cat needs care. Most veterinarians will talk to you for a few minutes at no charge, but even if you have to pay for an office visit, it's worth it to know that your cat's health—in fact, her life—will be in good hands.

You don't necessarily need to be friends with your vet, but you should be confident in his knowledge and skills. You should feel comfortable discussing your cat's care with him. He should listen to you and answer your questions. Above all, he should really like cats. If you don't like your vet or his approach to providing care, or if the atmosphere or policies of the practice in which he works make you uncomfortable, find someone else.

Routine Geriatric Examinations

Throughout her life, your cat should have routine examinations at least once a year, but as she grows older, your veterinarian may recommend more frequent checkups. Early detection is key in managing some of the problems that may come with age, and changes can occur quickly, so for most healthy seniors, six-month intervals between exams are about right.

At each routine visit, your vet will:
- examine the teeth and gums for tartar, swelling, or inflammation
- examine the ears for infection, ear mites, or other problems

Work in Partnership With Your Vet

You can help your veterinarian diagnose and treat problems your older cat may experience by observing and writing down physical or behavioral changes that you notice over time. The devil, as they say, is in the details, so write down the following information:
- when you first saw each physical or behavior change
- whether each condition or behavior is present all the time or only sometimes
- how often the condition or behavior occurs
- how long the condition or behavior lasts
- what was happening around your cat at the time

Cats-Only Vet Practices

As we all know, going to the doctor is stressful, and if your cat is unaccustomed to dogs or afraid of them, a waiting room full of canines can make vet visits even worse. If that's the case, consider switching to a cats-only practice.

- examine the eyes for pupil response and retinal health
- examine the skin and coat for parasites and other problems
- check weight, temperature, respiration, and heart rate
- draw blood samples for laboratory analysis
- examine a fecal sample to check for intestinal parasites

Vaccinations

The immune system can become less effective with the passage of time, making it less able to fend off disease without some help. On the other hand, vaccination— particularly overvaccination—

poses risks of its own. In fact, the American Veterinary Medical Association (AVMA), a number of veterinary colleges, and many veterinarians and pet owners have modified the way they vaccinate pets because of these risks. Despite this, it's important to remember that proper vaccination is still the best protection against infectious diseases that can kill and disable their victims.

Vaccines for cats can be divided into two types. Core vaccinations are considered essential for all cats to protect them against common diseases for which risk of exposure is high. Noncore vaccines, which protect against less common diseases, are optional, and the decision to give one or more of them depends on your cat's age, health

As your cat grows older, your vet may recommend more frequent checkups. Early detection is key in managing health problems that come with age.

Commonly Recommended Health Screenings for the Geriatric Cat

In addition to routine examinations, your veterinarian may recommend one or more of the following types of tests for your older cat.

- *Urinalysis*—A series of tests performed on a urine sample.

- *Blood count*—Any of several tests that evaluate the cellular portion of the blood.

- *Blood chemistry panel*—Tests that evaluate the chemicals, enzymes, proteins, hormones, waste products, and electrolytes in blood, often used to diagnose and monitor diabetes mellitus, liver disease, kidney disease, and other diseases.

- *FIV and FeLV testing*—Screening for feline immunodeficiency virus or feline leukemia.

- *EKG (electrocardiogram)*—Screening for heart disease and heart murmurs.

- *Thyroid testing*—Screening for thyroid hormone levels based on physical or behavioral symptoms, history of thyroid disease, and other risk factors.

- *Radiographs (X-rays)*—X-rays may be recommended if your cat has symptoms of lung, heart, kidney, liver, or gastrointestinal disease. A routine baseline radiograph of your cat's chest may be recommended while she is healthy for comparison in the event that she develops a problem later in life.

- *Ultrasound*—A noninvasive method used to diagnose various diseases of the abdomen and chest, and injuries to tendons and muscles.

- *Endoscopy*—Use of a tiny camera inserted into the patient for diagnosis or during surgery.

- *Pre-anesthesia screening*—Analysis of kidney and liver function and blood chemistry recommended for older cats prior to anesthesia, because certain diseases can affect the way anesthesia drugs affect the body.

status, breed, potential for exposure to the disease, and type of vaccine.

Vaccine manufacturers and the veterinary community don't always see eye to eye on proper protocols for vaccinating cats. The manufacturers almost always recommend that vaccinations be given annually. Many veterinarians and cat owners believe that annual boosters are unnecessary and may damage the animal's immune system. So what should you do?

Inform yourself about the risks of both diseases and vaccinations, talk to your vet, and then decide which vaccines you want your cat to have and how often. The American Association of Feline Practitioners (AAFP) recommends that core vaccines (other than rabies) be given every three years or more often if there is a higher-than-normal risk of exposure to a particular disease. Other factors to consider include age and health status, where you live, and whether your cat goes outdoors or is ever boarded.

As a responsible owner, you will play an important part in your senior cat's wellness program.

Most vaccinations were traditionally given by injection under the skin (subcutaneous) or into the muscle (intramuscular). However, concern about the high incidence of sarcomas (cancers) near injection sites in a small percentage of cats has led to the development of newer vaccines in nasal form.

Parasites and Your Senior Cat

Parasites threaten cats of all ages, but as your feline grows older, the effects of parasites on her body may be more

The Core Vaccinations for Cats

All cats should be vaccinated for the following:

- *Feline Panleukopenia (feline distemper)*: A widespread, potentially fatal viral disease. Most cats will be exposed to it at some time in their lives. Elderly cats who contract distemper often die.
- *Feline Rhinotracheitis*: A widespread viral disease that causes severe upper respiratory infection, which can kill an elderly cat. Vaccination won't prevent the disease, but it will reduce the severity of its symptoms.
- *Feline Calicivirus*: A viral disease that affects the upper respiratory system. It accounts for nearly half the upper respiratory infections in cats. Once a cat becomes infected, treatment has limited effect, and she may continue to carry the virus and suffer runny eyes and sneezing all her life.
- *Rabies:* A viral disease that devastates the central nervous system. Rabies is always fatal once symptoms appear, and it can attack any mammal, including people. It is transmitted in the saliva of an infected animal, often but not always by way of a bite. Rabies outbreaks occur fairly often in wild animals, which can pass the disease on to domestic animals. Prevention is the only cure for rabies.

According to the Centers for Disease Control (CDC), in the new millennium, the number of cases of rabies in cats has increased, while cases in all other domestic animals have decreased. Cats account for more than twice as many cases of rabies as do dogs or cattle. Rabies vaccination is required by law in most states (and in many other countries), and your cat should be vaccinated in compliance with your state law.

damaging. Let's look at the most common parasites that attack cats and see what you can do about them.

Fleas

Fleas are nasty little bloodsucking insects. They have hard shells that make them remarkably resistant to being squashed, and they are world-class jumpers, able to leap out of danger at a single bound. Fleas eat the blood of their victims and will prey on cats and other mammals, including people. There's no question that fleas are annoying, but they're much worse than that—fleas carry deadly diseases and parasites in their saliva, which they inject into their victims when they bite to keep the blood from coagulating.

Strategic prevention is the best approach to fleas, although there is no reason to keep your cat on a preventive year round if you haven't seen any fleas on your cat or in your

Are Herbal Flea Products Safe?

People sometimes assume that "all-natural" or "herbal" products are safe. In fact, plants are biological chemical factories, and the chemicals in them that repel or kill insects also can be toxic to humans and their pets. Other products may not be dangerous but simply ineffective and a waste of money. Unfortunately, herbal products are generally not categorized or regulated as pharmaceuticals. Before using any "natural" or "herbal" product on your cat, check with your veterinarian to be sure that it is safe.

program for your pets, home, and yard.

Ticks

Ticks are not insects; they are arthropods (relatives of spiders) that eat the blood of their hosts. They lurk in woods, fields, and grass, waiting until their heat sensors alert them to nearby prey. Then they grab onto fur or clothing until they can embed their pincher-like mouthparts in their victim's skin and begin feeding on blood. The tick's mouth is made to lock into flesh and will loosen its grip willingly only when it has finished feeding. Ticks, like fleas, carry diseases that affect both animals and people.

home or yard. If you do see a flea on your cat or elsewhere in your environment, you can be sure that it's not alone, so you must launch an eradication program as soon as possible. Fleas reproduce quickly, and to get rid of them, you have to kill them at all life stages: adult, larva, and egg.

Most over-the-counter products are only moderately effective, so you will probably spend less in the long run by spending a little more up front for better products from your vet. In addition, some flea products are hazardous for cats, and the chemicals in some of them can interact dangerously when used together. Your best bet is to speak to your vet about an effective prevention

Common Noncore Vaccinations for Cats

The American Association of Feline Practitioners (AAFP) recommends giving noncore feline vaccines to cats who stand a high chance of exposure to specific diseases through contact with other cats. Common noncore vaccines include those for feline leukemia (FeLV), feline infectious peritonitis (FIP), chlamydia, and ringworm.

55

Routine Health Care

Cats usually are not affected by ticks as badly as dogs, but I have pulled the occasional tick off my cats. If ticks are a problem where you live, inspect your cat at least weekly—more frequently if she goes outdoors, especially in warm weather. A fine-toothed flea comb can help you locate ticks under her fur.

If you find a tick that has attached itself, remove it carefully. Although pulling its head off has a certain appeal, you don't want to leave the head in your cat's skin, where it can cause infection. You can make the tick loosen its grip by dabbing it with a cotton ball soaked with iodine, alcohol, or a strong saline solution. Then, grasp the tick's body with forceps, tweezers, or your fingers with a tissue over them. (Or use a special tick remover, available from some pet-supply stores.) Pull gently and straight out. Don't squeeze the tick—you might force its body fluids into your cat (or yourself), increasing the chances of infection or disease. Dispose of the tick in a safe place.

Clean the bite with alcohol, Betadine, or iodine. After about five

Parasites threaten cats of all ages, but as your feline grows older, the effects of parasites on her body may be more damaging.

Toxoplasmosis

The Centers for Disease Control and Prevention (CDC) estimates that about one-third of people in the United States have been infected with toxoplasmosis, or "toxo." Most of us never know we've had the disease, which is a problem only when the victim is pregnant or immunosuppressed. Once infected, a person is immune.

Many cat owners express concern about acquiring toxoplasmosis from their cats, but the fact is that most cases come from eating or incorrectly handling raw or undercooked meat, especially pork. The only way your cat could transmit the *Toxoplasma gondii* parasite that causes toxo is in her feces, and only during the few weeks after she is first exposed to the disease. Cats cannot transmit toxoplasmosis by licking you or being petted. It takes 36 to 48 hours for the parasite's eggs in the cat's stool to become infective, so clean your cat's litter box at least once a day, and wash it once a week with soap or detergent and rinse it with scalding water. Wear gloves when you clean the litter box, and wash your hands with soap and hot water when you're finished.

If you are pregnant or plan to become pregnant, ask your doctor to test you to determine whether you have had toxoplasmosis. According to the CDC, a woman who tests positive for toxoplasmosis antibodies prior to becoming pregnant will not pass the parasite to her fetus. If you are not immune to the disease, have someone else clean your cat's litter box, and don't interact with stray or unknown cats.

minutes, apply antiseptic ointment. Wash your hands and any tool you used with soap and hot water. After you pull the tick out, you should see a small hole in the skin. A black spot indicates that you have left the head. Don't panic, but do keep an eye on the spot for a few days. If you see signs of infection, call your vet.

Ringworm

Despite its name, ringworm is not a worm but a highly contagious fungus. Ringworm spreads easily from one pet to another, and it is one of the few health problems that people get from their pets. For an elderly cat with a less-effective immune system, ringworm can be a threat not only in and of itself but as an opening for other infections that may enter through the raw, itchy skin.

The first symptom of ringworm is usually a sore-looking bald circle, but you should have your vet examine any bald spot on your cat as soon as possible. Like other fungal infections, ringworm is hard to treat effectively and even harder to cure. If you think that your cat has ringworm, don't waste your time and money on over-the-counter or home remedies. Your vet can make an accurate diagnosis and

A sudden or dramatic change in your cat's behavior or appearance may signal a health problem, so take her to the vet.

prescribe effective drugs. He also can advise you on how to keep the infection from spreading throughout your household.

Mange

Mange is the generic term for several skin conditions caused by various species of tiny arthropods called mites. They eat skin debris, hair follicles, and tissue, and cause severe itching, hair loss, and often a flaky crust on the skin. Animals with mange usually scratch themselves raw, making it easy for viral, fungal, or parasitic infections to take hold.

Three types of mange occur in cats:

• *Demodectic mange* occurs rarely, and it is thought that the cat's immune system must be compromised before the mites that cause demodex in cats can get a foothold.

• *Notoedric mange,* also known as sarcoptic mange or scabies, is cause by a microscopic mite that burrows beneath the skin to lay eggs. The eggs hatch in less than three weeks, and the larvae quickly develop into adult mites and begin to lay their own eggs. Scabies can cause extensive hair loss, and it can be passed back and forth by cats, dogs, and people.

• *Cheyletiella mange* is also known as "walking dandruff" because the mites

Not All Heartworm Medications Are the Same

Both cats and dogs are vulnerable to heartworm, and both need preventive medication. However, the dosage requirements are very different in the two species. Do not treat your cat with your dog's heartworm medicine, or vice versa.

that cause it look like dandruff on the animal's head, neck, and back. Although unattractive and highly contagious, cheyletiella is the least serious of the manges because it is easy to treat and is short-lived.

Treatment for mange varies with the type of mite, so if you suspect that your cat has mange, see your vet. Be sure to ask whether you need to treat your other pets or take any special precautions for human members of the family.

Internal Parasites

Cats are subject to several species of parasitic intestinal worms. Some create no problem at all and pretty much go unnoticed, but others can

threaten your cat's health, especially in higher concentrations or when combined with old age or disease. The following are the common intestinal worms found in cats.

Roundworms

Roundworms (ascarids) are white spaghetti-like creatures about 8 inches (20 cm) long. They don't attack the host animal directly but eat food passing through the animal's digestive system. Roundworms are carried by many species of animals and are easily acquired, especially if your cat spends time outdoors and kills and eats prey animals. Roundworms can cause nausea, vomiting, diarrhea, and anemia, and a large infestation can cause malnutrition. Fortunately, roundworms are easy to diagnose and treat.

Better prevention, treatment, and pain control can all work together to help make your cat's senior years healthier, happier, and more plentiful.

Symptoms That Require Veterinary Attention

Some signs of illness require a quicker response than others, especially when observed in an older cat. If your cat has one or more of the following symptoms, contact your veterinarian.

- abnormal aggression
- bleeding or discharge
- blisters or ulcers on the tongue
- continual sneezing
- coughing
- dehydration
- depression
- diarrhea
- difficulty breathing or breathing through the mouth
- difficulty urinating or defecating
- fever
- frequent urinary "accidents" or a change in the color, odor, or amount of urine
- discharge from nose and eyes
- lameness or stiffness that lasts more than a day or two
- listlessness
- loss of appetite or difficulty eating, drinking, or swallowing
- lumps or swellings that persist or grow larger
- offensive or unusual odor
- paralysis
- reduced stamina
- sores that do not heal
- unexplained weight loss or gain
- vomiting
- watery eyes
- weakness

Tapeworms

Tapeworms are segmented white worms that can grow to enormous lengths in the host's intestines. The tapeworm begins its development in an intermediate host, and your cat must eat the intermediate host along with the worm larvae it harbors. The larvae then mature in their new host—your cat. Common intermediate hosts include fleas, mice, rabbits, and other animals. Tapeworms do not normally show up in feces, making them more difficult to diagnose than most other worms. But they do shed small, white, rice-like body segments that are passed in bowel movements and that often stick to the fur around the anus. If you see tapeworm segments on your cat, talk to your vet. A special dewormer is needed to eliminate tapeworms.

A number of other parasites also can take up residence in your cat. Aside from direct evidence, signs of intestinal parasites may include weight loss, anemia, respiratory infection, and diarrhea. If your cat has these symptoms, see your vet, and take a fecal specimen along. Even if your cat has no symptoms of worms, it's a good idea to include a fecal exam as part of her routine examinations.

Heartworms

Heartworms are devastating for a cat of any age, but especially so for an older cat. These long, thin parasitic worms are carried in larval form from infected

Learn More About Alternative Veterinary Medicine

To learn more about alternative veterinary medicine and to locate links to many sources of information about the individual fields, visit:
www.listservice.net/wellpet/
www.altvetmed.org
www.holisticvetpetcare.com

animals to new victims, and they may affect cats, dogs, and even people. Symptoms of heartworm infection vary widely, from no symptoms at all to vague signs of poor health to coughing and other signs of congestive heart disease. Without treatment, an infected cat may die of heartworm disease.

Heartworms are spread by mosquitoes, which ingest the microscopic larvae when feeding from infected animals and then pass the larvae to new victims. The larvae then travel through the animal's blood vessels to the heart, where they take up residence and reproduce, damaging the cardiovascular system and eventually leading to congestive heart failure.

Even if your cat never goes outdoors, she is at risk if you live in heartworm country, which includes most parts of North America. You can protect her with regular doses of a heartworm preventive that kills the

61

Better prevention and treatment can make your cat's senior years more comfortable.

microscopic larvae before they can mature into life-threatening adult heartworms. Monthly preventives are available in pills and in topical forms applied to the skin, and some of them also prevent intestinal parasites or fleas. These drugs are highly effective, but no medication is perfect, so even if your cat is on a heartworm preventative, your veterinarian may suggest testing her every year or two during her regular examination to be sure that she is heartworm free. Speak to your veterinarian about the best preventive program for your cat.

Alternative Therapies

Over the past several decades, some veterinarians and pet owners have embraced nonconventional approaches to preventive care and treatment for animals. Variously classified as alternative, complementary, or holistic medicine, these alternative approaches all seek not only to relieve symptoms of disease, but also to identify, and if possible, eliminate the source of the problem. They hold in common the belief that physical and emotional factors together affect an animal's health.

Some practitioners of alternative approaches to pet health care are formally trained in veterinary medicine and related fields, including chiropractic, acupuncture, homeopathy, herbal therapy, and nutrition. Others, however, have no training in the science of animal health and could harm your cat either directly or by delaying effective treatment. In addition, although some treatments are effective for some animals, the claims made for others have never been verified through scientific research. The bottom line about alternative veterinary care? Be cautious.

Veterinary medicine has come a long way over the past several decades—and that's good news for your cat and for you. Better prevention, treatment, and pain control can all work together to help your cat's senior years be healthier, happier, and more plentiful.

Chapter 5

Managing

Age-Related Changes

With age comes change. Some changes will occur gradually and will cause you and your cat few if any problems—graying hair, less activity, and so forth. Other changes, especially those related to acute or chronic illness, may affect your cat's health or behavior in more distressing ways. In either case, knowing what to expect and what options you have will make the process easier on both of you. It's important to recognize common changes that you may see as your cat grows older.

Gastrointestinal Changes

As the years go by, most of us find that we can't eat like we used to. The same goes for older cats, who often lose their ability to digest and absorb fat. As a result of this digestive change, combined with the loss of subcutaneous (under the skin) fat and muscle tone, your aging cat may gradually lose weight and take on an "old and bony" feel. Some weight loss is okay for most cats, but being too thin can compromise your pet's overall health. A change in diet may help keep body weight normal, and some older felines do better with several small meals a day rather than one or two big ones. To monitor your cat's food intake and increase her interest in food when it's available, feed meals rather than leaving food out. (See "Free Feeding Versus Scheduled Feeding" in Chapter 3.) Weight loss also can indicate a health problem, so if your cat is losing weight, speak to your veterinarian.

Many older cats experience constipation for a number of reasons. Digestion tends to take longer in an older cat than in a young one, and that slows the bowels. If your cat has arthritis or an impacted or infected anal gland, defecation may cause her pain and she may avoid "doing her duty" as long as possible.

Another common cause of constipation in cats of all ages is the infamous hairball. You can help to

Major Problems in Older Cats

- arthritis
- cancer
- confusion or memory loss
- diabetes
- heart disease
- impaired hearing, vision, or other senses
- kidney disease
- liver disease
- obesity
- oral disease
- poor coat or skin

prevent hairballs by brushing your cat frequently to remove hair that she would otherwise swallow. Hairball treatments, often in the form of a tasty paste, can help. Special foods are also available now that are supposed to prevent hairballs from forming.

Some older cats don't drink enough water, especially if they have to walk very far to get to it, and insufficient water intake can lead to dehydration and constipation. Make it easier for your old friend by placing a source of clean drinking water in an easily accessible area. If your cat has chronic bowel problems, or if she fails to eliminate for more than a day, contact your veterinarian.

Your older cat also may experience diarrhea from time to time. In most cases, loose stools indicate nothing more than a mild tummy upset, and a bland diet will usually clear it up in a day or so. You may have to experiment to find something your cat will eat; try plain yogurt, cottage cheese, boiled chicken, unsalted chicken broth, bread soaked in unsalted broth, or boiled rice, alone or in some combination. However, diarrhea can quickly weaken and dehydrate an elderly cat, and it also may point to a more serious problem. If you are in doubt or if your cat has diarrhea for more than two days, if her stools contain blood, or if she also

Knowing what changes to expect as your cat ages and what care options you have will make the process easier on both of you.

Medicine or Poison?

Some drugs that are generally safe for people and dogs can kill your cat, even in small doses. Don't give your cat any medication unless a veterinarian specifically instructs you to do so.

vomits or has a fever, see your vet immediately and, if possible, take a stool specimen for analysis.

Changes in Skin, Coat, and Claws

Older cats often show signs of advancing age in changes in their fur and skin. Good food will provide the nutrients essential to maintaining a healthy "outer cat." (See Chapter 3, and keep in mind that your cat's nutritional requirements may change with time.) Good regular grooming, especially brushing, will help to stimulate circulation and the oil glands, and it will distribute the natural oils that lubricate the coat and skin. (See Chapter 4.) Still, expect some changes to occur as part of the natural aging process.

One of these changes may be the appearance of white or gray hair, especially on your cat's face—unless, of course, she is white or gray. Her coat also may become thinner, and the texture of her hair may change. These changes may simply be signs of advancing age, but they also may indicate a nutritional deficiency or disease. If you see a sudden or significant change in your cat's coat, see your vet. If the change has been gradual and your cat seems healthy, mention the change in her coat during her next regular exam.

Your cat's skin will also change over the years, becoming thinner, drier, less elastic, more delicate, prone to injury and infection, and slower to heal. Use grooming sessions to check for lumps, bumps, irritations, or sores, and get veterinary help with anything out of the ordinary before it becomes a serious problem.

Your cat's claws also may change over the years, becoming drier and more brittle. Again, nutrition or disease could be to blame, so check with your vet. In any case, check your cat's feet and nails frequently, and if she has stopped using her scratching post, help her by trimming her nails as needed. (See Chapter 4.)

Arthritis and Muscular Changes

Many cats, especially those who have suffered joint injuries when younger, develop arthritis as they age. In some cases, it causes only mild stiffness; in others, it causes debilitating pain. If your cat no longer jumps or climbs as she once did or looks stiff or sore as she moves, talk to your veterinarian. Great strides have been made in

Cats often tend to hide their illnesses, so if you suspect that your pet is sick, take her to the vet right away.

Take Your Medicine, Dear

"Pilling the cat" may seem almost as difficult as belling her, but as your cat grows older, you may need to medicate her at times. You may be able to camouflage the medicine in something tasty, like canned cat food, human baby food, or some other soft treat. The trick with this approach is to be sure that your cat gets the whole dose. If so, congratulations! If your cat is too sly to fall for that trick, you'll have to take the direct approach.

- Sit or kneel where you can hold your cat comfortably and securely. If someone else can hold her while you administer the medicine, that's even better. If your cat resists being restrained, wrap her fairly snugly in a towel or small blanket with just her head sticking out. Most cats relax a bit when wrapped, so you will have better control. Have the medicine ready and within reach.

- Place the palm of your hand on top of her head, with the index finger and thumb of the same hand at either corner of her mouth. Gently tilt her head back. Her mouth will probably open slightly by itself. If it doesn't, push gently down on her lower incisors with the middle finger of your other hand.

- If you are giving a pill, drop it as far back on your cat's tongue as you can. (If you don't like to put your fingers in her mouth, purchase a pill plunger from your vet, pet supply store, or pharmacy.) Keep your cat's head tilted back, and massage her throat or blow lightly on her nose until you're sure that she has swallowed.

- If you are giving a liquid medication, get an oral syringe with measurements marked on the side from your vet or pharmacy. This simple tool will make it easier to measure the dosage and to get it safely down your cat's throat. Insert the syringe between her cheek and teeth, and slowly depress the plunger. Don't squirt it straight down her throat—she may choke.

- Hold your cat for a minute or two after you give the medicine. Stroke her and talk to her, and give her a special treat if she'll take one. When she relaxes, let her go. If you let her leap away immediately after taking the medicine, you will just reinforce her opinion that taking medicine is a horrible thing, and the next time will be even more difficult.

Keep an eye on your cat for a while after you give her the medicine. Cats vomit easily and at will, and you want to be sure that she doesn't purge herself of the stuff you just put down her throat. If she does throw up the medicine, do not give her anymore until the next scheduled dose unless you're sure she lost the whole dose. If she repeatedly throws up her medication, ask your vet about alternatives.

FAMILY-FRIENDLY TIP

Older Cat Etiquette

Arthritis and loss of vision and hearing can make it difficult for your older cat to keep herself safe from fast-moving kids. If your child is old enough to be mobile but too young to understand your cat's limitations, then it's up to you to be sure that your cat is out of harm's way. Older children should be taught to be aware of where the cat is and to move slowly and handle her gently to avoid startling or hurting her. If she is able to exercise gently, your child may enjoy tossing a toy for short, supervised exercise sessions. If your cat can't hear, teach children to move into her line of sight before touching her, and if she can't see, teach them to speak to her as they approach. Most importantly, teach them to leave her alone if she's sleeping or if she doesn't want attention.

difficult (and painful, if your cat has arthritis), she will move less, lose more muscle, and reduce her movements even more. You get the picture. Not only will lack of movement and muscle loss be self-perpetuating, but insufficient exercise can harm your cat's heart, digestive system, and emotional health as well.

Moderate exercise, on the other hand, is important to your cat's health even into advanced old age, and you can encourage her to keep moving in several ways. If she has difficulty moving around, try placing some simple, secure ramps leading to her favorite chair or perch. Play with her gently, tossing toys or crumpled paper for her to chase or swat. Give her empty paper bags and boxes to explore.

If your cat is unable to exercise even that much, you can stimulate her circulation and help her joints and muscles stay supple by flexing and massaging them gently every day. She will probably enjoy the attention and stimulation—if not, she will tell you. If that's the case, just pet her gently, talk to her, and relish the time you still have with her. Love, after all, is the best medicine.

Changes in Your Cat's Heart, Lungs, Kidney, and Liver

Even with the best nutrition, exercise, and proper health and dental care, certain changes to your

pain relief over the past few years, and your vet may suggest nutritional supplements or prescribe anti-inflammatory or pain medications to reduce your pet's discomfort.

Your cat's muscle mass and tone may diminish with age as well, which may lead to a vicious cycle of declining health. As movement becomes more

If your cat is unable to exercise, you can stimulate circulation and help her joints and muscles stay supple by flexing and massaging them gently every day.

an electrocardiogram (EKG) or echocardiogram to diagnose a heart problem. If your cat is diagnosed with heart disease, the symptoms may be controllable with medication.

Age also takes a toll on the lungs, making them less elastic and limiting their ability to oxygenate blood. The result is usually reduced stamina and a higher susceptibility to respiratory problems, especially if your cat has asthma. Older cats are also more likely to contract infectious respiratory diseases, so your vet may recommend changes in your senior's vaccination schedule.

The kidneys also become more vulnerable to disease over time due both to natural changes that occur as the body ages and to other health

cat's internal organs are inevitable as she grows older. Let's see what you can expect and what you can do to prevent or manage problems that may occur as a result.

Like your cat's other muscles, her heart will lose muscle tone and become less efficient with age. Cardiomyopathy, a disease of the heart muscle, is fairly common in elderly cats. Depending on your cat's age, general condition, and symptoms, the veterinarian may simply listen to her heart with his stethoscope, use radiographs (X-rays), or recommend

More Help for the Diabetic Cat

If your cat has diabetes, you can help to maintain her blood sugar and weight at proper levels by keeping her indoors so that you have control over everything she eats. Just be sure that everyone who might feed her knows that she can't have extra goodies!

problems, including gum disease and heart problems. Symptoms (usually increased drinking and urination) do not usually appear until kidney disease is well advanced, so most vets recommend screening for proper kidney function through urinalysis or blood chemistry analysis as part of the regular physical exam and before any procedure that requires anesthesia. Medication and a special diet may control kidney disease, especially if you catch it early.

The job of the liver is to remove toxins from the blood and to produce certain proteins and enzymes. Infections, parasites, cancer, toxins, medications, and a number of diseases all can cause potentially fatal damage to the liver, especially in an older cat whose liver is less efficient than it was when she was younger. Jaundice is commonly associated with liver disease, but because other symptoms are not specific, liver disease can be difficult to diagnose. Nevertheless, most vets recommend screening for proper liver function as part of routine geriatric care and before anesthesia.

Glandular Changes
Older cats may suffer from hormone-related diseases caused by glandular

The Expert Knows

Pain Control
Cats are generally reluctant to let on when they are in pain, and because they often hide their suffering, pain was often left untreated in the past. Happily, over the past decade, veterinarians and owners have become more sensitive to the issue of pain in ill, injured, and post-surgical animals, and safer, more effective medications have become available. If your cat is ill or injured or has had surgery, don't let her suffer in silence. Ask your vet about pain control.

changes that occur with advancing age. Again, most vets recommend routine screening for hormone levels in the blood because early intervention with diet, drugs, and other treatments improve the odds of effective control of these diseases. Let's look at some of the more common glandular problems seen in older cats.

Diseases of the Pancreas
The pancreas produces several enzymes that are essential for processing sugars and fats in the diet.

Diabetes Mellitus
Diabetes mellitus occurs when the

pancreas loses its ability to metabolize and regulate blood sugar through the production of insulin. Symptoms of diabetes include heavy water consumption, and consequently, heavy urination. Obesity can lead to diabetes, but not all diabetic cats are fat. If your cat drinks and urinates a lot, or if she is overweight, consider having her tested for diabetes.

Some cases can be managed with changes in diet, but many diabetic cats require daily insulin injections to control excess blood sugar. If that is true for your cat, your vet can teach you to give the injections at home and to monitor blood sugar with urine glucose strips available from any pharmacy. He also can explain what to do if your cat's blood sugar drops too low from the insulin injections. Even with careful home care and monitoring, you will need to take your cat to the vet frequently to be sure that her insulin dosage is correct.

Pancreatitis

Pancreatitis is a potentially fatal inflammation of the pancreas. Symptoms include fever, abdominal pain, and elevated heart rate. Eating too much fatty food can bring on an attack of pancreatitis, or it can be caused by certain infections, medications, metabolic disorders, trauma, or shock. If your cat is diagnosed with pancreatitis, your vet will probably advise you to withhold food for a short period to give the pancreas a chance to rest and recover. He also may administer fluids and

Sudden weight loss or weight gain can indicate a number of different health problems, so seek veterinary advice.

electrolytes to combat dehydration and may prescribe other treatments to manage potential complications or to address the suspected cause of the pancreatitis.

Thyroid Disease

Hyperthyroidism—the overproduction of thyroid hormone—is not uncommon in feline seniors. It is, in fact, the most common endocrine problem in cats. Environmental, nutritional, and immunological factors are all thought to contribute to the development of tumors that stimulate the thyroid glands to secrete too much thyroid hormone.

Although the symptoms of hyperthyroidism vary from one cat to another, some are common. The majority of hyperthyroid cats lose weight despite increased appetites, and many exhibit heart murmurs or elevated heart rates. Other common symptoms include vomiting, excessive thirst and urination (which also may indicate diabetes), and increased activity. Initial diagnosis can be complicated, though, because some cats have less appetite and become less active as they age. In some cases, an affected cat may experience diarrhea or respiratory problems.

Blood tests that assess hormone levels are necessary to accurately diagnose hyperthyroidism. Once diagnosed, the disease usually can be controlled with drugs, radioiodine therapy, or surgery.

Vomiting

Most of the time, vomiting does not mean that your cat is really ill. A simple upset tummy, a hairball, or stress can cause your cat to upchuck. On the other hand, vomiting can indicate a serious health problem. Your cat needs to see her veterinarian immediately if:

- there is blood, worms, or foreign objects in her vomit
- she also has diarrhea, or abdominal swelling or pain
- she vomits repeatedly
- she repeatedly vomits white or clear fluid
- she is listless

Anal Glands

Like most predators, your cat has anal glands (anal sacs) embedded in her anal sphincter muscle. When the animal defecates, or becomes alarmed or excited, the glands excrete a pungent fluid that identities the individual animal. It is, in fact, the presence of that fluid that makes an animal's feces so interesting to other animals.

Healthy anal glands are expressed, or emptied, every time your cat has a bowel movement. Anal glands can, however, retain fluid if they become impacted (blocked), infected, or injured, which can cause your cat discomfort, pain, and in some cases, more serious complications. If you notice your cat licking or biting excessively at her anal area or scooting her fanny across the floor, or if she develops a foul odor, she needs veterinary attention. Treatment usually involves manually expressing the glands, a simple procedure. In chronic cases, the glands can be removed.

Mammary Tumors

Mammary tumors are fairly common in older female cats, especially those who have experienced one or more heat cycles or who have had kittens. Some feline mammary tumors are benign, but unfortunately, the majority of tumors are cancerous. Surgical removal, sometimes followed by additional therapy, is successful in certain cases.

If your cat is female and has not been spayed, or if she was spayed after coming into heat or bearing kittens, your vet should examine her mammary glands as part of her regular checkup.

Can You Hear Me Now?

Many older cats lose some or all of their hearing, but if you have other pets, your hard-of-hearing cat may fool you by using visual clues from the rest of the family. Our cat Mary was completely deaf before we realized that she'd lost her hearing;

I discovered it when we were in a room alone without the other animals. Loss of hearing also may be mistaken for aggression, because if your cat doesn't hear someone approaching, she may be startled and respond reflexively with a swat or bite. Give her the benefit of the doubt, especially if the "nasty" behavior is new. Try to determine whether she can hear, or talk to your vet.

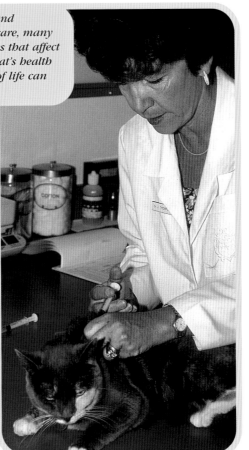

With timely and appropriate care, many of the changes that affect your senior cat's health and quality of life can be managed.

Warning Signs That May Indicate Disease

You are your cat's best protection against disease. If you notice any of the following symptoms in your cat, have her examined by your veterinarian as soon as you can. Early diagnosis may save or extend her life and protect her from unnecessary pain.

Hyperthyroidism:
- increased appetite
- increased drinking and urination
- increased activity
- rapid heart rate (pulse)
- rapid or labored breathing
- repetitive vomiting
- unexplained weight loss

Kidney or Bladder Disease:
- black, tarry stool
- blood in urine
- blood in vomit
- depression
- diarrhea
- difficulty urinating
- increased drinking and urination
- lethargy
- urinating outside the litter box

Inflammatory Bowel Disease:
- diarrhea
- loss of litter box habits
- more frequent defecation
- mucus or blood in stool
- unexplained weight loss
- vomiting

Diabetes Mellitus:
- change in appetite
- decreased activity
- increased drinking and urination
- unexplained change in weight
- vomiting
- walking on hocks (the joint between the long bones of the upper and lower hind leg)
- weakness

Heart Disease:
- exercise intolerance
- paralysis of rear legs
- rapid or labored breathing
- unexplained weight loss

Cancer:
- bleeding or discharge
- difficulty breathing
- difficulty eating or drinking
- difficulty urinating or defecating
- lethargy or lack of stamina
- loss of appetite
- persistent unpleasant odor
- sores that do not heal
- swelling anywhere on the body
- unexplained weight loss

Liver Disease:
- depression
- diarrhea
- distended abdomen
- loss of appetite
- pale or yellow gums
- unexplained weight loss
- vomiting

Hearing loss due to aging is usually permanent. You can't buy your cat a hearing aid, but you can do a few simple things to make life easier for both of you. Even if she cannot hear voices or the whir of the can opener, she may hear sharp sounds or sense vibrations. Try clapping your hands, stomping on the floor, or tapping gently on the chair where she's lounging. Visual signals are also effective with many deaf cats. Try moving into her field of vision or flashing a light to get her attention. Lack of hearing puts your cat at serious risk outdoors, so keep her inside where she's safe.

Eye and Vision Changes

Changes in the appearance of the eye and partial or complete blindness are not uncommon in elderly cats. Your cat's eyes may develop a cloudy bluish look due to nuclear sclerosis, a normal change that doesn't always affect vision. Other changes in the eyes can be more problematic, though —cataracts, glaucoma, and other eye diseases can affect vision and potentially lead to other problems. If the appearance of your cat's eyes changes suddenly, or if she bumps into things or no longer watches moving objects, talk to your vet.

Cancer

Feline lymphoma is a common cancer of cats. It can affect different organs

In Case of Emergency...

Pets 911 runs a toll-free phone hotline (1-888-PETS-911) that allows pet owners access to important, life-saving information. You can also visit their website at: http://www.1888pets911.org.

but always involves lymphoid cells. Feline lymphoma is more common in cats that have FeLV or FIV.

Remission and life expectancy in cats with lymphoma depend on the location of the tumor(s) and how soon the disease is found and treated. Chemotherapy can increase life expectancy in affected animals, and radiation or surgery also may be used in some cases. Most cats live four to six months with treatment, four to six weeks without.

Other cancers also affect cats, so have your vet examine any sores that don't heal or unexplained lumps you find on your cat. Cancer treatment is a rapidly evolving field, so if your pet is diagnosed with cancer, you may want to consult a veterinary oncologist for the most up-to-date options.

Change is inevitable. As your cat grows old, her body will respond to the passage of time, not always in ways you would choose. Still, with good, timely care, many of the changes that affect her health and quality of life can be managed.

Chapter 6

Managing Age-Related

Behavior
Changes

Age alters not only the body but the mind and emotions as well, and as your cat grows older, you may see some changes in her personality and behavior. Some of these will occur so gradually and make so little difference that they will go unnoticed. You may even welcome some of her new behaviors and be glad to see the end of a few old ones. Who could regret the disappearance of little furry gifts at the back door, or "Supercat" swinging from the top of the living room drapes?

Other changes are not so welcome. Some of the health problems and physical changes that were discussed in the last chapter can affect your cat's personality, behavior, and sleep patterns in negative ways, and elderly cats are often less able to handle stress than they were when younger. Pain, disease, nutritional deficiencies, food allergies and sensitivities, medications, and stress all can contribute to inappropriate elimination, aggression, fears and phobias, and other new and undesirable behaviors.

As we have seen, regular home and veterinary health care and good nutrition play vital roles in keeping your cat physically, mentally, and emotionally healthy in her golden years. Physical exercise and mental challenges are also important components of a healthy, happy life.

The Twin Fountains of Youth: Play and Exercise

George Bernard Shaw said, "We do not stop playing because we grow

Exercise Can Help Your Older Cat

Regular exercise, as approved by your veterinarian, is good for your aging cat. It will help her live a longer and healthier life by:

- channeling and boosting her energy
- controlling some emotional effects of aging
- helping to control her weight
- keeping her joints strong and flexible
- keeping her mind active
- strengthening her heart and lungs
- toning and strengthening her muscles

old. We grow old because we stop playing." This is as true for cats as it is for people, and although you can't stop the march of time, you can slow some of its negative effects on your cat by keeping her as active as she can be for as long as possible.

How Much Should Your Cat Sleep?

Sometimes it may seem as if all your cat does is sleep, especially as she grows older and sleeps longer and more soundly. Cats do sleep a lot—about 16 hours a day is normal in an adult. (That's twice as long as most mammals spend sleeping.) So long hours in the sack should not worry you, but sudden or extreme changes in your cat's sleep patterns could be cause for concern. If you notice such a change, talk to your vet.

And yes, your cat undoubtedly dreams, as shown by her movements and her brain wave patterns, which are similar to the patterns of your own brain waves when you dream. Wouldn't you love to know what she dreams about?

As your cat grows older, you may see some changes in her personality and behavior.

Regular, moderate exercise will help to keep your cat's aging joints limber and strong. It will strengthen and tone her muscles, maintain her at a proper weight, increase her energy level, help her sleep better, strengthen her cardiovascular system, and keep her internal organs strong and healthy. Just as important, play and exercise will fend off boredom, keep her mind sharp, and help to prevent the emotional shifts that all too often accompany old age. And here's a big bonus: Playing with your cat will make you feel better, too, and will help to keep the bond between you strong.

As your cat enters her senior years, she won't, of course, need as much exercise as she did as a kitten and young adult. But barring a health problem that precludes activity, she does need to do more than toddle to the food bowl and litter box a few times a day. Unfortunately, she may be less willing to self-exercise than she used to be, so it's your job (and, I hope, your pleasure!) to find ways to encourage your cat to move around. The good news is that the best exercise is play. Forget the burn—just encourage your cat to play with you.

Granted, getting an adult cat to play can be a challenge, particularly if she's been spending most of her time in sedentary pursuits like eating, grooming, and sleeping. The challenge may be compounded if your cat has a physical limitation; poor hearing or vision, for instance, may make it more difficult to engage her interest. With a little imagination, though, you can probably get her up and moving. Remember, no matter how sweet and pretty and cuddly, your cat is a hunter at heart. Appeal to her predatory instincts with toys that move and that make high-pitched squeaky sounds.

You can spend a fortune on really cute toys that you find irresistible but that may or may not appeal to your cat. Some of the best cat toys are the simplest, cheapest things. Chances are you already know what your cat likes,

but in case you need some new ideas, here are a few simple "toys" that have gotten my cats moving over the years:

- crumpled sheet of paper
- empty cardboard toilet paper or paper towel roll
- empty boxes of various sizes
- empty paper grocery bags (no plastic, please—your cat could suffocate)
- plastic tops from milk jugs or other containers
- small, clean, empty plastic bottle
- a small plastic bottle with a few small stones inside
- small foam rubber or soft plastic balls
- a strip of polar fleece with one or two knots tied in it

These inexpensive—and sometimes free —toys can promote lots of fun.

Barring a health problem that precludes activity, an elderly cat still needs daily exercise to stay physically and mentally healthy.

How to Deal With Unwanted Behaviors

Sometimes, older cats who have been well behaved for many years suddenly start doing things their people don't much like. Some such behaviors are merely annoying, but others are serious problems for cat and owner alike. It's important to understand, though, that some feline behaviors you don't like are normal and make perfect sense to your cat. (And to be fair, a lot of things you do must look very odd to your cat!) In addition, an elderly cat may behave in certain ways because she is in pain or ill. It's your job to try to figure out what's going on and to do what you can to make it easier for your feline friend to do what you want her to do.

If your cat just doesn't seem to be her old self, or if she begins to behave in an unusual or undesirable way, begin by checking for an underlying medical cause. Give your veterinarian as much information as possible about what your cat does and when she does it—details can make a diagnosis easier. If your vet finds no physical cause, and if he rules out nutritional problems, take a close look at your home from your cat's perspective. Sometimes a small change in the environment can make a big difference in behavior.

Many age-related behavior changes can be managed through veterinary intervention, environmental adjustments, or behavior modification techniques.

Health Conditions That Can Affect Housetraining

If your previously reliable cat stops using her litter box some or all of the time, take her to your veterinarian for a checkup. A variety of medical conditions can cause older cats to develop inappropriate elimination behaviors, including:

- arthritis
- colitis
- diabetes mellitus
- feline lower urinary tract disease (FLUTD)
- hyperthyroidism
- impacted or inflamed anal sac
- inflammatory bowel disease
- kidney or liver disease
- vision problems

(See Chapter 5 for more information.)

Now, let's look at some of the behavior changes that older cats display.

Housesoiling (Inappropriate Elimination)

The most commonly reported behavioral problem in aging cats is inappropriate elimination—pottying outside the litter box. Although this behavior may take many forms, most often the cat deposits urine or feces outside the litter box some or all of the time. When a previously clean and reliable cat develops such behavior, it is especially disturbing.

A once well-behaved senior may unexpectedly misbehave or act strangely because she is ill or in pain.

Health problems, including disease, injury, chronic or acute pain, food sensitivities, or intestinal parasites, can cause your cat to change her litter box habits. Any physical factor that causes urination or defecation to be painful, or that makes getting in and out of the litter box painful or difficult, can lead to the soiling behavior. Among these are feline lower urinary tract disease (FLUTD), kidney or liver disease, colitis, bowel or anal sac disease, hyperthyroidism, diabetes mellitus, arthritis, or vision problems. If your cat begins "tinkling outside the box," your first step should be to see your vet to rule out or treat any physical problem.

Another common trigger for a change in potty habits is stress. Many older cats don't handle stress well, and things that your cat once took in stride may bother her as she ages. Stress can be brought on by many factors, including illness or pain, a change of residence, a new household routine, the addition or loss of people or pets in the household, or other factors. Obviously, you cannot eliminate change or stress—both are part of life. But with a little planning and attention, you can minimize their effects on your cat. Simply providing a safe and private refuge, ensuring that some things remain "normal," and spending time with her can significantly lower her stress level.

The first thing you need to do is to figure out why your cat's behavior has changed. And you need to do so quickly, because the longer the behavior continues, the more difficult it will be to change it. But why would your once fastidious feline suddenly forget where to go? Let's look at some common causes of inappropriate elimination.

As your cat ages, her urinary and digestive systems may prompt her to

be the source of the problem. For instance, the idea of an "odor-reducing" or "private" or "self-cleaning" litter box may appeal to you, but your cat may prefer her old-fashioned plain old box.

Strong odors in particular can drive a cat out of the box, like scented litter, scents put into the air near the litter box, or residual odors from soaps and detergents. They all may smell nice to you, but may overpower and offend your cat.

Have you changed the type of litter you use? Some cats are quite fussy about their litter and refuse to use one with a different texture from what they are used to. Have you increased or

Who Goes There?

If you have more than one cat and find urine outside the litter box, ask your vet for an edible dye that will color urine. Give it to each cat, one at time, to find out who is using the box and who is not.

use the litter box more frequently. No one likes a dirty potty, so you may need to clean the box more frequently. If you are gone for long hours and cannot clean it more than once a day, consider providing an extra litter box. If your cat has arthritis, getting to the litter box and in and out of it may be painful. A simple change, such as a more accessible location, boxes on different floors of your house, or a box with lower sides, may solve the problem.

Remember, though, that cats—particularly older cats — are not amused by what they see as unnecessary changes. If your cat's habits changed after you "improved" her facilities for reasons of your own—perhaps switching to a different type of box or litter—that change could

An aging cat's urinary and digestive systems may prompt her to use the litter box more frequently or may cause inappropriate elimination.

reduced the amount of litter you put in the box? If your cat is used to having more or less, she may be frustrated by the change. Have you started using plastic litter box liners? Your cat may not like them. If you have moved to a new home or rearranged your current one, your cat may dislike the location of the litter box and decide not to use it. Is it near her food and water? Even cats don't like to potty where they eat and drink. Can your dog intrude on your cat when she uses the litter box? That may discourage her. Have you

Not-So-Lonely Times

If you have to leave your cat alone for long periods, there are a few things you can do to relieve her loneliness:

- Leave a radio or television on. The sound of music and voices soothes many animals.
- Provide secure, comfortable spots for your cat to look out the window. Provide a chair or couch, or a wall-mounted perch. Activity on the street or in your garden can provide lots of entertainment.
- Spend some time with your cat when you get home, and if possible, before you leave. If she's able to play, give her some exercise. If not, do a little grooming, massaging, or petting.

added another cat to the family? Some felines don't like to share their boxes.

If your cat does begin to go outside her litter box, you need to act quickly, before the bad habit is ingrained. Cats have sensitive noses and can locate a "bathroom" even where you smell nothing, so be sure to remove all trace of waste using a cleaner made to remove organic odors.

Whatever you do, don't punish your cat for lapses in litter box training. She will just lose her trust in you, and if you don't address the source of the problem, she will likely continue the behavior more slyly. Identifying the cause of the behavior and making it easier for her to be right will be much more effective.

Anxiety

Older cats, like many older people, do not handle stress as well as they did when younger. If she's ill, arthritic, or losing her vision or hearing, your cat will be even more susceptible to anxiety brought on by everyday life. Stress and anxiety can lead to many behavioral problems, including aggression, hiding, inappropriate elimination, changes in appetite, obsessive self-grooming or lack of grooming, and obsessive chewing or sucking on cloth, toys, and other things. You can't eliminate stress from your cat's life, but you can help her cope with it.

The first step is to figure out what's bothering your cat. First, be sure that

Older cats do not handle everyday stress as well as they used to, which can lead to problems such as aggression, hiding, and phobias.

earlier in this chapter, play is good for body and soul, so play with your cat if she is still up to it. Groom her frequently, even if only for a few minutes a day. Even if she sleeps a lot and doesn't come looking for you as much as she used to, she still needs quality time with you. Treasure the moments you have.

Animals react in widely diverse ways to old age and infirmity, and if she doesn't have a medical or physical condition that can cause her stress. Obesity or malnutrition, injury, chronic pain, surgery or other veterinary treatment, illness, and parasites all can affect your cat's emotions and behavior. Loneliness, death or absence of a family member (human or animal), or the arrival of a new person or pet in the household may upset your cat.

Once you think that you have identified the source of your cat's anxiety, remove it if you can. If that isn't possible, provide your cat with a refuge from it, and try to minimize the effects. Don't let people or other pets disturb her when she wants to be alone, but be sure to spend time interacting with her. As we saw

FAMILY-FRIENDLY TIP
Kids and Pet Stress

Young children lack the ability to anticipate the results of their own actions or to empathize with other creatures. If your cat has lost her vision or hearing, she will be surprised more easily. If she is no longer able to move quickly, she is likewise more vulnerable than when she was younger. Placing your older cat at the mercy of a young child can be disastrous for both, increasing your cat's stress level and subjecting her to possible pain or injury, and putting your child at risk of being swatted as your cat defends herself. Interaction between children and pets always should be supervised, but this is especially critical for an elderly animal or a young child.

you have other pets, their reactions to your older cat may bother her. Kittens (as well as other young animals, and children) are often oblivious to the limitations and desires of an elderly cat. Adult cats and dogs may be concerned and gentle with an older cat, or they may seize on her waning abilities to bully or even hurt her. Young children who are not yet able to empathize with other living beings or to comprehend the possible results of their actions also can be a problem for a cat who is no longer able to get away easily. If you think that another pet or a young child is causing your cat to be anxious,

Some seniors develop separation anxiety because they become insecure as they realize that their senses aren't what they used to be.

try giving her a part of the house to herself temporarily, or if necessary, permanently.

Some older cats suffer from long-standing fears and become afraid of things that didn't used to bother them, such as thunder, vacuum cleaners and other appliances, and outside noises such as motorcycles, garbage trucks, and lawn mowers. A moderate level of fear or anxiety is not unusual and is not normally a cause for concern, especially if your cat recovers quickly.

Remember, too, that your response to whatever frightens your cat, and to her behavior, can influence her. Remain calm and reassure her. Be sure, too, that you don't inadvertently reward and encourage her fearful behavior. It's fine to pet her and talk reassuringly, but don't overdo it. She may interpret your snuggling and baby talk as a reward for her fear. Just talk calmly, stroke her occasionally (if she's not under the bed!), and go about your business.

If your cat shows fear that seems out of proportion to the thing or event, or if she seems to be afraid of "ghosts," talk to your vet. New treatment options, including drugs, environmental "calming hormones," and behavioral approaches, are being developed all the time. If she seems likely to injure herself or someone else during a panic attack, you might want to confine her to a plastic cat carrier for safety. Put it in a quiet place, and your cat will probably feel safe and calm down.

Separation Anxiety

Separation anxiety is a specific type of anxiety in which an animal suffers extreme stress during her owner's absence. Separation anxiety can result in undesirable behaviors, including inappropriate elimination, loud vocalizing, or excessive and self-destructive grooming. Separation anxiety also can cause physical

The Expert Knows

What Causes Separation Anxiety?

The likelihood that your cat will develop separation anxiety is probably influenced by her genes, environment, and life history. Kittens who are orphaned or weaned too early seem to be especially prone to this problem. A major change in environment, such as a move to a new home or the addition or removal of a family member, also can make your cat insecure and lead to separation anxiety, as can illness.

symptoms, including stress-induced diarrhea, vomiting, or anorexia. In most cases, symptoms and behaviors appear 8 to 12 hours after the owner leaves, although some cats become anxious much more quickly. Some develop separation anxiety late in life, perhaps because they are ill or in pain, or because they feel insecure as they realize that their senses aren't what they used to be.

Anxiety or Phobia?

Moderate fear or anxiety is not usually a big problem for you or your senior cat. But if her fear becomes irrational or excessive, she may have developed a phobia, and you may need to work with your veterinarian or a behaviorist to find an effective treatment.

Health Conditions Can Cause Aggression or Anxiety

Even if your cat does not appear to be ill or in pain, certain medical conditions can cause or increase aggressive behavior, including hormone imbalances and disease of the internal organs. Pain or anxiety caused by such conditions can make the situation even worse. If your cat becomes aggressive, schedule a thorough veterinary exam to rule out physical causes.

Separation anxiety can be treated, but success requires time, patience, and effort. Making a fuss when you leave and when you return can reinforce any notion that your cat has about your departure and absence being bad, so try to come and go quietly and calmly. Talk to your cat, but don't make a big deal of it right before you leave or right after you arrive.

If your cat is still active and playful, giving her some interesting toys and treats may distract her from your absence. Have one or two special toys that you give your cat when you leave and pick up when you get home. Hide a few tasty treats in different places around the house for your cat to find while you're gone.

Many people swear by alternative approaches such as herbal treatments, TTouch, acupuncture, and so on to calm an anxious cat. (See Chapter 4.) More conventional anti-anxiety medications are also useful in extreme cases, so if you can't ease your cat's mind by simpler means, ask your vet about short-term drug therapy. And of course, check with your vet before giving your cat any alternative treatment to be sure that it won't interact negatively with any other medications she takes or with the condition she has.

Aggression

Some cats, like some people, get cranky as they grow old. Most of the time, the

If your cat's unusual behavior continues or worsens, schedule a thorough veterinary exam to rule out physical causes.

crabby behavior is not threatening, but occasionally it blooms into aggressive actions aimed at people and other pets. An aggressive cat is no fun to live with, and seeing a once sweet pet behave that way can be heartbreaking. It also can be dangerous.

A cat whose personality changes in this way is not a happy feline. Aggressive behavior that begins in old age is usually a response to pain or fear. Chronic pain from arthritis or long-term illness, or acute pain from injury or disease, can cause your cat to lash out. She also may bite or scratch in self-defense if she is frightened by pain or startled because she is losing her hearing or vision. Finally, many diseases can trigger chemical changes that affect your cat's mind, causing behavioral changes, including aggression.

If your cat gets crotchety, tell your vet about the problem and have him give your cat a thorough physical exam. If a medical problem is at the root of the aggression, ask about treatment options. If your cat seems to be healthy, ask for a referral to a qualified animal behaviorist who is experienced with feline aggression. Whatever you do, don't meet aggression with violence. Hitting, kicking, or throwing things at your pet won't solve the problem and will almost certainly make her more fearful and aggressive.

Keep in mind, too, that it is easy to mislabel an unexpected but perfectly

Helping Your Vet
Make a Diagnosis

You rely on your veterinarian for the medical knowledge that can help to keep your cat healthy and longer lived. But your veterinarian also depends on you. After all, you're the one who can observe your cat as she lives her normal life. Here are some ways you can help your vet help your cat:

- Take your cat in for regular physical examinations at least once a year, more often if recommended due to her age or condition.

- Feed your cat a quality food suited to her health status.

- Monitor your cat's weight, and don't let her become obese or too thin.

- Groom your cat regularly, and check her over for lumps, cuts, inflammations, sore spots, and other signs of trouble.

- If you notice an unusual condition or behavior, write down information that may be significant—when you first noticed it, how often it occurs, and other factors that may be important.

- See your vet promptly if your cat is ill or injured—the sooner a problem is diagnosed, the better the chance that treatment will be successful.

reasonable action as "aggressive." If your cat's behavior is infrequent, and if there is an obvious reason (she was startled, or someone stepped on her tail, for instance), then there's probably no cause for concern. Who wouldn't hiss and swat under those circumstances? Respect her desire to be left alone, and teach children to do the same. After all, she's old—she's earned it.

Learn to recognize warnings. Cats rarely bite or swat without warning, but people often fail to get the message in time. If your cat growls, twitches her tail or skin, stiffens her body, flattens her ears back, or unsheathes her claws, she's flashing a feline red light.

Regardless of her reasons, if she becomes aggressive, your first priority should be to keep people and other animals safe. Those sharp claws and teeth can cause serious, permanent injuries in a heartbeat. If you cannot get a handle on aggressive behavior very quickly by yourself, seek professional help.

The passage of time will undoubtedly cause behavioral changes in your aging cat. Some of them will be insignificant to the overall quality of your relationship. Some will even make your feline companion dearer to your heart. And some may be unwelcome. With continuing love and care, though, most behavior changes can be managed, and you and your cat can continue to share love and affection throughout her golden years.

It's your job to figure out what's causing your senior's change in behavior and to do what you can to make things easier for her.

Chapter 7

A Fond Farewell

Saying goodbye to a beloved pet is one of life's most difficult experiences, and our cats' relatively short lives are the sad price we pay for the joy of having them as companions. With good care and a measure of good luck, your cat may remain healthy well into her teens, but eventually her advancing age will take its toll. Fortunately, we are able to offer our pets the final loving gift of a gentle passage with dignity and freedom from pain.

The Hardest Decision

The decision to euthanize is never easy to make. You will undoubtedly consider a number of factors before you make a choice that is right for your cat, yourself, and the other members of your household.

Your cat's overall quality of life should be the first and most important factor you consider. Unless she is in acute pain, you will probably have some time to consider your options, and if you pay attention, chances are your cat will give you the answer herself. Does she seem to be depressed or in pain most of the time? Has she become withdrawn? Has she lost interest in interacting with other members of the household or in simple pleasures like cuddling or eating? If your cat's bad days outnumber the good ones, it's time to discuss euthanasia with your veterinarian.

Talk to your vet about your cat's condition, treatment options, and chance for recovery. Of course, she cannot "recover" from being old, but if a medical problem can be treated, your cat may be able to live comfortably and happily a bit longer. Realistically, not all illnesses can be treated effectively, and cost may be a factor. You shouldn't feel

Your cat's overall quality of life should be the first and most important factor you consider as she advances in age.

guilty or embarrassed if you can't afford to treat your cat's serious or chronic illness, especially if it offers only a few months of respite.

Long-term care for a very ill animal also can take an emotional toll on you and other members of your household, including other pets. If your cat requires frequent or special treatments, or becomes incontinent or unable to move around, her care can become a physical challenge for the caretaker, and unless someone is home most of the time, scheduling treatments may be very difficult. Being realistic about what you can and cannot provide doesn't make you a bad person or bad pet owner. In fact, confronting reality is more responsible than ignoring it. You'll likely get opinions from other people, so remember that what would be right for someone else may not be right for you. Be honest with yourself and with your vet about your capacity to manage the financial, physical, and emotional costs of special or long-term care for your pet.

If your cat is terminally ill but you're not ready to let go, you may want to look into home hospice care. Some veterinary hospitals and organizations now offer this service, keeping the animals comfortable in their own homes and giving family members time to come to terms with their impending loss. If you are interested in learning more about veterinary hospice care, ask your vet or contact your closest vet

Hospice Care for Terminally Ill Pets

The American Association of Human-Animal Bond Veterinarians (AAH-ABV) offers information on home hospice care for terminally ill animals. Visit the website at www.members.aol.com/guyh7/hospice.htm, or ask your veterinarian for more information.

school, or see the web links provided in this chapter.

If you decide that it is time to let your cat go, talk to your vet about where and when the euthanasia procedure will take place. Some vets will come to your home, especially if you're a long-time client and your cat is very ill. If you plan to take your cat to your vet's office, try to schedule a time when the clinic is less busy and when you won't have to rush back to work or to other obligations. Be kind to yourself as well as to your cat, and allow yourself time to grieve and to reflect on the time you had with your feline friend.

You should decide ahead of time who will be present. Everyone should have the opportunity, before and after euthanasia has been performed, to say goodbye, and talking about it in advance will make it easier for everyone when the time comes. Young children probably should not witness the euthanasia process, but they should

A Fond Farewell

The Stress of Losing a Pet

Psychologists confirm that losing a pet is one of the most stressful events we can experience. Take time to mourn, and look into grief counseling if you feel overwhelmed by your sadness. Take good care of yourself and of others who loved your cat. Your cat would want you to.

few cats and dogs, and the pain of losing them was eased a little by seeing that they went gently and with dignity, in the arms of the people who loved them.

The euthanasia process is fast and virtually painless. Your vet may shave some fur from your cat's leg to make the vein more accessible, and he may give a preliminary sedative. Then he will inject concentrated pentobarbital directly into a vein, causing the heart to stop in a matter of seconds. Sometimes the body moves slightly after that as the muscles relax. In addition, the lungs may expel air, and the bladder and bowels may empty. Be assured that your cat is already gone and feels no pain.

be prepared for the loss of their pet, and they should have a chance to say farewell and to express their grief. If you or other family members want some time alone with your pet after the procedure to say a final farewell, tell your vet.

Knowing what to expect also will make the process less frightening. Over the years, I've said farewell to quite a

Ensuring that your cat enjoys her final years in comfort and peace is the best thanks you can give for her many years of loyalty and companionship.

FAMILY-FRIENDLY TIP

Helping Children Through the Loss of a Pet

Children understand death and deal with it differently at different ages. The Association for Pet Loss and Bereavement (APLB) offers information and resources for helping a child through the grieving process on its website or by telephone or mail. See the "Resources for Managing Grief" sidebar in this chapter.

If you simply cannot face being present, that's understandable. You're not abandoning your kitty but placing her in gentle hands that will guide her on her way. But if you can, your cat will be more at ease if you hold her, stroke her, and talk to her while the injection is given. Your friends and family will probably give you all sorts of advice, but only you can decide what is best for you and your cat.

Speak to your vet ahead of time about how you want your cat's body handled. You may want to have her cremated individually and have the ashes returned to you to keep, bury, or scatter in a special place. Or you may choose to have her cremated

with other pets, in which case the ashes will not be returned. Many communities have pet cemeteries where you can have your cat buried. If you want to bury her at home, make sure that it is legal where you live, and lay chicken wire over the body to prevent wild animals from digging up the grave. Whatever you want to do, your vet can help you make the arrangements.

Dealing With Your Loss

Losing a beloved cat is a painful experience. Be kind to yourself. Plan for something to do for the rest of the day, and avoid people who don't understand. This was not "just a cat," as some people might say. She was your cat, and she shared your life and love. Pity anyone who tries to belittle your feelings, and surround yourself with those who understand.

Holding a small ceremony, alone or with family or friends, may help you deal with your loss and give you a sense of closure. Pet memorial services are not just for children. You might want to bury your cat's remains (check your local laws first) or her ashes, or her collar or favorite toy. When we lost our beautiful orange tabby, Leo, my husband and I buried him and planted cat mint over his grave.

To begin healing, you and other people who loved your cat may need to talk through their feelings. If you don't know anyone with whom you

A Fond Farewell

Resources for Managing Grief

For information about pet loss grief counseling services, contact the Association for Pet Loss and Bereavement (APLB), P.O. Box 106, Brooklyn, New York, 11230, telephone (718) 382-0690, or at www.aplb.org.

can express yourself comfortably, consider contacting a grief counseling service or joining a pet-loss support group on the Internet or in your community. (See the resources in this chapter.) There you will find understanding and helpful suggestions.

Photo albums and scrapbooks are also wonderful ways to commemorate your relationship with your cat. An assortment of photos, and perhaps cartoons or poems or other pieces that make you think of her, can bring your happy memories to the fore and help you rejoice in the life she lived and the good things she brought to your own life.

Surviving Pets and Loss

Human friends of your cat are not the only ones who will experience loss and grief at her passing.

If you have other pets, they too will react emotionally to your cat's death. And if she had a special friend, that animal may experience profound grief. When my Leo died, our dogs moped around for several days, sniffing Leo's favorite spot on the couch frequently and apparently looking for him in his usual spots.

If you have other cats, the dynamics of the group may change with the loss of one of the group members. Even if everyone gets along, you may see a little jockeying for social status within the group, and you may see adjustments in who hangs out with whom. These changes usually resolve themselves in a few days. Occasionally, a pet's grief turns into deep depression.

Photo albums and scrapbooks are wonderful ways to commemorate your relationship with your cat.

Positive Ways to Channel Your Sorrow

Although grief is a very personal emotion, many people find that it is eased by turning it into action focused on others. An excellent way to honor your cat is to help other animals in her name. Here are some ideas to consider for memorial donations; you will know what feels right to you.

- A local animal shelter.

- A cat rescue organization. (Visit www.kittysites.com/rescue.html for an extensive list of shelters and rescue organizations.)

- A feline health research project or organization (especially if your cat died of a disease for which a cure is being sought). Find more information at www.winnfelinehealth.org.

- An organization that backs disaster relief for animals. Find more information at www.avmf.org and www.noahswish.org.

- An organization that supports the human–animal bond. The Delta Society certifies therapy cats and offers more information at www.deltasociety.org. The Center for the Human-Animal Bond at Purdue University offers information on research, education, and service programs on its website at www.vet.purdue.edu/depts/vad/cae/.

- An organization that helps people through the grief of losing a pet.

The Rainbow Bridge

Just this side of Heaven is a place called Rainbow Bridge. When an animal dies that has been especially close to someone here, that pet goes to Rainbow Bridge. There are meadows and hills for all of our special friends so they can run and play together. There is plenty of food and water and sunshine, and our friends are warm and comfortable. All the animals who had been ill and old are restored to health and vigor; those who were hurt or maimed are made whole and strong again, just as we remember them in our dreams of days and times gone by.

The animals are happy and content, except for one small thing: They miss someone very special to them who had to be left behind. They all run and play together, but the day comes when one suddenly stops and looks into the distance. The bright eyes are intent; the eager body quivers. Suddenly she begins to break away from the group, flying over the green grass, her legs carrying her faster and faster. You have been spotted, and when you and your special friend finally meet, you cling together in joyous reunion, never to be parted again. The happy kisses rain upon your face; your hands again caress the beloved head, and you look once more into the trusting eyes of your pet, so long gone from your life but never absent from your heart.

Then you cross Rainbow Bridge together.

– Author unknown

[*The Rainbow Bridge* is an inspirational poem that tells the story of where pets go when they die. Created by an unknown author, it has comforted many pet lovers grieving the loss of their beloved companions.]

If you have other pets, they too will react emotionally to the loss of their feline friend and may experience profound grief.

This is most common when the deceased is survived by an animal with whom she spent most of her life, or with whom she was especially close. Depression is signaled by abnormal withdrawal from normal activities, lethargy, and sometimes loss of appetite. If you see symptoms of depression that last more than a few days in one of your surviving pets, speak to your vet. A short course of antidepressant medication may help.

Remember that not only do you take comfort in your time of sorrow from your remaining pets, but they also take comfort in you.

Pet Grief Counseling

Petloss.com is a website devoted to pet loss grief support. It offers extensive resources such as referrals to online and local support groups; grief counseling by phone; a monitored message board and chatroom; inspirational books, articles, and poetry like Rainbow Bridge; tribute pages; a weekly pet loss candle ceremony; and much more.

Resources

Registry Organizations

American Association of Cat Enthusiasts (AACE)
P.O. Box 213
Pine Brook, NJ 07058
Phone: (973) 335-6717
Website: http://www.aaceinc.org

American Cat Fanciers Association (ACFA)
P.O. Box 1949
Nixa, MO 65714
Phone: (417) 725-1530
Website: http://www.acfacat.com

Canadian Cat Association (CCA)
289 Rutherford Road South
Unit 18
Brampton, Ontario, Canada L6W 3R9
Phone: (905) 459-1481
Website: http://www.cca-afc.com

The Cat Fanciers' Association (CFA)
1805 Atlantic Avenue
P.O. Box 1005
Manasquan, NJ 08736-0805
Phone: (732) 528-9797
Website: http://www.cfainc.org

Cat Fanciers' Federation (CFF)
P.O. Box 661
Gratis, OH 45330
Phone: (937) 787-9009
Website: http://www.cffinc.org

Fédération Internationale Féline (FIFe)
Penelope Bydlinski, General Secretary
Little Dene, Lenham Heath
Maidstone, Kent, ME17 2BS ENGLAND
Phone: +44 1622 850913
Website: http://www.fifeweb.org

The Governing Council of the Cat Fancy (GCCF)
4-6, Penel Orlieu
Bridgwater, Somerset, TA6 3PG UK
Phone: +44 (0)1278 427 575
Website:
http://ourworld.compuserve.com/homepages/GCCF_CATS/

The International Cat Association (TICA)
P.O. Box 2684
Harlingen, TX 78551
Phone: (956) 428-8046
Website: http://www.tica.org

Traditional and Classic Cat International (TCCI)
(formerly known as the Traditional Cat Association)
10289 Vista Point Loop
Penn Valley, CA 95946
Website: http://www.tccat.org

Veterinarian Specialty/Membership Organizations

American Animal Hospital Association (AAHA)
P.O. Box 150899
Denver, CO 80215
Phone: (303) 986-2800
Website: http://www.aahanet.org

American Association of Feline Practitioners (AAFP)
200 4th Avenue North, Suite 900
Nashville, TN 37219
Phone: (615) 259-7788
Toll-free: (800) 204-3514
Website: http://www.aafponline.org

American Holistic Veterinary Medical Association (AHVMA)
2214 Old Emmorton Road
Bel Air, MD 21015
Phone: (410) 569-0795
Website: http://www.ahvma.org

American Veterinary Medical Association (AVMA)
1931 North Meacham Road, Suite 100
Schaumburg, IL 60173
Phone: (847) 925-8070
Fax: (847) 925-1329
Website: http://www.avma.org

The Academy of Veterinary Homeopathy (AVH)
P.O. Box 9280
Wilmington, DE 19809
Phone: (866) 652-1590
Website: http://www.theavh.org

The American Association for Veterinary Acupuncture (AAVA)
P.O. Box 419
Hygiene, CO 80533
Phone: (303) 772-6726
Website: http://www.aava.org

ASPCA Animal Poison Control Center
1717 South Philo Road, Suite 36
Urbana, IL 61802

Telephone: (888) 426-4435
www.aspca.org

International Veterinary Acupuncture Society (IVAS)
P.O. Box 271395
Ft. Collins, CO 80527
Phone: (970) 266-0666
Website: http://www.ivas.org

Animal Welfare Groups and Organizations

American Humane Association (AHA)
63 Inverness Drive East
Englewood, CO 80112
Phone: (800) 227-4645
Website: http://www.americanhumane.org

American Society for the Prevention of Cruelty to Animals (ASPCA)
424 East 92 Street
New York, NY 10128
Phone: (212) 876-7700
Website: http://www.aspca.org

Best Friends Animal Sanctuary
Kanab, UT 84741-5001
Phone: (435) 644-2001
Website: http://www.bestfriends.org

Cats Protection
17 Kings Road
Horsham, West Sussex RH13 5PN UK
Phone: +44 (0) 1403 221900
Website: http://www.cats.org.uk

105

Resources

Feral Cat Coalition
9528 Miramar Road, PMB 160
San Diego, CA 92126
Phone: (619) 497-1599
Website: http://www.feralcat.com

The Humane Society of the United States (HSUS)
2100 L Street, NW
Washington, DC 20037
Phone: (212) 452-1100
Website: http://www.hsus.org

The Winn Feline Foundation, Inc.
1805 Atlantic Avenue
P.O. Box 1005
Manasquan, NJ 08736-0805
Phone: (732) 528-9797
Website:
http://www.winnfelinehealth.org

Websites

Acme Pet Feline Guide
(http://www.acmepet.com/feline/index
.html)
A leading figure in the pet products
industry, Acme Pet has put together an
extensive site. At the feline site, you can
access the feline marketplace, which
has places to shop for cat products as
well as a pet library, reference materials
and articles, questions and answers
about cats, an extensive list of rescue
organizations, clubs and shelters, and
the ever popular "cat chat" room.

ASPCA Animal Poison Control Center
1717 South Philo Road, Suite 36
Urbana, IL 61802

Telephone: (888) 426-4435
www.aspca.org

Cat Fanciers Website
(http://www.fanciers.com)
In 1993, the Cat Fanciers mailing list
was started on the Internet as an open
forum for breeders, exhibitors, judges,
or anyone interested in the world of
the Cat Fancy. The on-line discussion
group has thousands of members from
all over the world. The group's focus,
however, is to make life better for
felines around the globe. The site offers
general information on cat shows,
breed descriptions, veterinary
resources, and much more.

The Daily Cat
(http://www.thedailycat.com)
The Daily Cat is a resource for cats and
their owners. The site provides
information on feline health, care,
nutrition, grooming, and behavior.

Healthypet
(http://www.healthypet.com)
Healthypet.com is part of the American
Animal Hospital Association (AAHA) an
organization of more than 25,000
veterinary care providers committed to
providing excellence in small animal
care.

Petfinder
(http://www.petfinder.org)
On Petfinder.org, you can search over
88,000 adoptable animals and locate
shelters and rescue groups in your area
who are currently caring for adoptable
pets. You can also post classified ads for

lost or found pets, pets wanted, and pets needing homes.

Pets 911
(http://www.1888pets911.org)
Pets 911 is not only a website; it also runs a toll-free phone hotline (1-888-PETS-911) that allows pet owners access to important, life-saving information.

ShowCatsOnline
(http://www.showcatsonline.com)
ShowCatsOnline.com is an online magazine devoted to all breeds of pedigreed cats. They provide information on the breeding and showing of all breeds of pedigreed cats and update their members on the latest developments in medical care, breeding, grooming, and showing.

21cats.org
(http://21cats.org)
21Cats provides information that will help cats live longer, healthier lives. The site contains an online Health and Care InfoCenter, an "Ask the Kitty Nurse" Hotline, and a free monthly newsletter. One of their goals is to raise awareness of successful methods used to reduce the cat overpopulation problem.

VetQuest
(http://www.vin.com/vetquest/index0.html)
VetQuest is an online veterinary search and referral service. You can search their database for over 25,000

veterinary hospitals and clinics in the United States, Canada, and Europe. The service places special emphasis on veterinarians with advanced online access to the latest health care information and highly qualified veterinary specialists and consultants.

Publications

Animal Wellness Magazine
PMB 168
8174 South Holly Street
Centennial, CO 80122

ASPCA Animal Watch
424 East 92nd Street
New York, NY 10128

Cat Fancy Magazine
P.O. Box 52864
Boulder, CO 80322

Catnip
P.O. Box 420070
Palm Coast, FL 32142

CatWatch
P.O. Box 420235
Palm Coast, FL 32142

Whole Cat Journal
P.O. Box 1337
Radford, VA 24143

Your Cat Magazine
1716 Locust Street
Des Moines, IA 50309

Resources

Index

Note: Boldface numbers indicate illustrations.

Senior Cats

111

Index

About the Author

Sheila Webster Boneham, Ph.D., is a life-long cat lover with a special soft spot for senior felines. Her work has appeared in national publications, including *Cat Fancy* and publications of the Cat Fanciers' Association. In 2003, the Cat Writers' Association honored Sheila's book *The Complete Idiot's Guide to Getting and Owning a Cat* (Alpha Books) with an Award of Excellence and the MUSE Award for Best Care and Health Book. She lives in Indiana with her husband and her furry friends.

Photo Credits

Trevor Allen (Shutterstock): 52, 88; Joellen L. Armstrong (Shutterstock): 102; Carlos Arranz (Shutterstock): 98; Joan Balzarini: 75; Anne Gro Bergersen (Shutterstock): 15; Carolina (Shutterstock): 64; Claudia Carlsen (Shutterstock): 46; Hermann Danzmayr (Shutterstock): 78; Lindsay Dean (Shutterstock): 100; Lakis Fourlakis (Shutterstock): 103; Isabelle Francais: 19, 20, 39, 58, 73, 85; Carlos Gauna (Shutterstock): 44; Stefan Glebowski (Shutterstock): 7; Johanna Goodyear (Shutterstock): 13, 37; Ralf Herschbach (Shutterstock): 91; Ingret (Shutterstock): 63; JC (Shutterstock): 32; Cheryl Kunde (Shutterstock): 12; Alexander Remy Levine (Shutterstock): 14; Gillian Lisle: 71; Torsten Lorenz (Shutterstock): 56; Jeff Oien (Shutterstock): 35; Robert Pearcy: 30, 34, 60, 82, 84, 90; Mark William Penny (Shutterstock): 59; Perrush (Shutterstock): 16; Michael Pettigrew (Shutterstock): 11; Robert Redelowski (Shutterstock): 29; K. D. Roedema (Shutterstock): 94; Ronen (Shutterstock): 40; Jean Schweitzer (Shutterstock): 4, 8; Jennifer Sekerka (Shutterstock): 93; Vincent Serbin: 67; Vaide Seskauskiene (Shutterstock): 96; Krasimir Stoyanov (Shutterstock): 53; Yanfei Sun (Shutterstock): 43; Denis Tabler (Shutterstock): 51; TFH archives: 21, 24, 81, 92; Ho Ying Tian (Shutterstock): 62; HTuller (Shutterstock): 15; John Tyson: 23, 27, 68, 87; Simone van den Berg (Shutterstock): 101; Carla van Wagoner (Shutterstock): 49; Zhorov Igor Vladimirovich (Shutterstock): 76